American Elites

ROBERT LERNER
ALTHEA K. NAGAI
STANLEY ROTHMAN

American

Elites

Yale University Press   New Haven and London

Designed by James J. Johnson and set in ITC Berkley Roman and Copperplate Gothic types by The Composing Room of Michigan, Inc.

Printed in the United States of American by BookCrafters, Inc., Chelsea, Michigan.

Library of Congress Cataloging-in-Publication Data

Lerner, Robert, 1953–

    American elites / Robert Lerner, Althea K. Nagai, Stanley Rothman.

      p.   cm.

    Includes bibliographical references and index.

    ISBN 0-300-06534-5 (alk. paper)

    1. Elite (Social sciences)—United States.   2. Social surveys—United States.   3. United States—Social conditions—1980– .

I. Nagai, Althea K., 1954–   .   II. Rothman, Stanley, 1927– .

III. Title.

HN90.E4L47   1996

305.5′2′0973—dc20   96-16343

A catalogue record for this book is available from the British Library.

10 9 8 7 6 5 4 3 2 1

DEDICATION

To Josh

BOB LERNER AND ALTHEA NAGAI

To Bessie Kopel
my favorite (and only) mother-in-law

STANLEY ROTHMAN

Contents

PREFACE

This book presents an analysis of the results of an intensive study of twelve major elites in American society.[1] Aside from the scope of study, the care with which the samples were chosen, the questionnaire, the use of the Thematic Apperception Test, and the relatively high response rate provide a detailed portrait of key American leadership groups not available elsewhere. The inclusion of various cultural elites like those responsible for motion picture and television entertainment adds another unique dimension. All respondents were interviewed personally. The response rate of most of the groups was over 60 percent; several were over 80 percent.

The empirical material, in addition to enabling us to understand better these leadership cadres, provides the basis for examining various theories of American society (elite theory, new class theory, and so on) as well as making some predictions about the future course of social and political development.

Readers familiar with the other studies Rothman has completed with various collaborators are aware that this volume is one of a series of books designed to help understand social change in our society. Additional volumes, both empirical and theoretical, will follow, including several designed to place our findings in social and historical context. The books thus far published include *The Media Elite* (1986) on news reporting, followed by *Watching America* (1992) and *Prime Time* (1994) on television entertainment, *The Mass Media and Democratic Societies* (1993), *Giving for Social Change: Foundations, Public Policy, and the American Political Agenda* (1994), and *Molding the Good Citizen: The Politics of*

High School History Texts (1995). The theoretical historical analysis underlying the various studies will be presented in *Elites in Conflict* (forthcoming).

Inspiration for the studies comes in large part from political scientist Harold Lasswell and sociologist Daniel Bell. As early as the 1950s Lasswell maintained that the key strategic elites (leadership groups) of the twentieth century would increasingly be those concerned with the creation and distribution of symbols for either knowledge or entertainment (Lasswell and Lerner, 1952). Bell made a similar point and also sketched the impact of such elites on American society (Bell, 1973, 1976). His argument, which we accept, is that certain key changes in American society have produced a cultural elite (broadly defined), which has become a significant critic of bourgeois society and is contributing in important ways to transforming its values and replacing them with new ones.

The studies undertaken have been designed to test the hypotheses advanced by Bell, Lasswell, and others and to explore further the complex nature of elite structure in American society.

Chapter one examines the history of elite theory in sociology and political science and the conflicting analyses of the role of elites in the United States.

In chapter two, we look at the data on the social background of American elites collected by Stanley Rothman and S. Robert Lichter, in light of the various propositions raised by the "class versus elite," and "power versus plural elites" debate that dominate the literature. Chapter two shows that American leadership groups are not a power elite, but are a system of multiple, competing, strategic elites.

In chapter three, we show the lack of a common upper-class system of values. While there is much value consensus within strategic elite groups, American elites are ideologically polarized. This chapter sets out four distinct dimensions of liberalism that divide American elites.

Chapter four shows the impact of ideology on how elites view the world around them. Ideology is a cultural system. It affects how respondents perceive the influence of various institutions such as religion, the military, and the government; how they choose long-term, broad-gauged goals for the whole society; how they evaluate various media (*The New York Times*, television news, PBS, etc.); and, of course, how they vote in Presidential elections. It encompasses much of how elites view social, economic, and political life in America.

Chapters five, six, and seven change the focus, shifting from the impact of ideology, to the social and familial correlates of ideology. In chapter five, we show that political socialization plays an extremely important role in the formation of contemporary elite beliefs. Fathers' liberalism makes one more supportive of collectivist liberalism. Chapter six discusses expressive individualism, which is less influenced by parents' values, than by current religiosity. We focus on how church attendance, not religious affiliation per se, is associated with one's *conservatism* regarding such social issues as abortion, adultery, and gay rights.

Chapter seven explores the adversary culture hypothesis we advance in earlier chapters: namely, that it is a composite of system alienation and regime threat. Taken together, the alienation and regime threat factors make up the ideology of the adversary culture.

Chapter eight examines the personality correlates of ideological adherence. We compare various elites in terms of such variables as the need for achievement, the need for power, and the fear of power. The scoring systems designed to measure these variables were empirically derived by David McClelland (1961, 1975), David Winter (1973), and many others. We find that one's need for achievement and one's need for power have significant effects upon one's choice of careers and political ideology.

Chapter nine draws together our results supporting the notion of strategic elites and ideological polarization, and examines some of their implications.

Aside from chapter eight, which is the most difficult in the book, technical details have been kept to a minimum, though they have not been eliminated. Even that chapter (and of course the others) can be understood by those who lack training in statistics, if they are willing to make just a bit of extra effort, though many of them will have to accept, on faith, our discussion of why certain statistical measures rather than others were used.

Funds for this particular book were provided primarily by the Donner Foundation; the Scaife and the Earhart foundations also provided generous assistance. The book could not have been completed without the key assistance of Jinny Mason, a Jill of all trades, who (given her political disagreements with us) helps keep us honest.

We also wish to thank Dr. Timothy Shortell, statistician/consultant, at the Jahnige Center at Smith College. At Rothman's request, Shortell reviewed our statistical analysis, knowing nothing about the study or our hypotheses. We, in turn, knew nothing about his social and political perspectives and still do not. His involvement was a check on our work by a neutral observer.

Dr. Shortell also suggested an alternate mode of analysis for several variables to clarify the presentation of the data. In several cases his advice was followed. He bears no responsibility, however, for the final results or for the interpretation of the data.

As with our other work, the questionnaires and tapes for this study will be deposited in the Roper Center at the University of Connecticut so that other scholars can examine our data beginning three years from the publication of this book.

Stanley Rothman
  Northampton, Massachusetts
Robert Lerner and Althea Nagai
  Rockville, Maryland

ONE

THE FEW VERSUS THE MANY: COMPETING VIEWS REGARDING THE STRUCTURE OF POWER

Any study of American elites must begin with a hotly debated issue: the relation between money and power in American life. Are American elites, especially the corporate elite, merely offshoots of the upper class, which in the last analysis rules the United States? Alternatively, is the Marxist and neo-Marxist notion of class rule simply untrue?

To answer these questions, we start by comparing the notion of an upper class and an elite group, both conceptually and empirically. We begin with a critique of the class domination model of American society, comparing the model with the more fruitful concept of "strategic elites." We then look at the work of Vilfredo Pareto, Gaetano Mosca, and Robert Michels, the classic elite theorists, followed by an examination of the writing of more recent theorists, most notably C. Wright Mills and Thomas Dye. Modern elite theorists argue that power in America is concentrated in the hands of a few. Plural elites theorists, however, criticize the unitary-elite model of American power as being empirically untrue.

A CRITIQUE OF UPPER-CLASS RULE IN AMERICA

Theorists searching for the American upper class argue that the United States is ruled by an upper economic class—a small, relatively stable group, of which leaders in government, business, and culture form a part. These class theorists believe that power ultimately rests in ownership of capital, which is still controlled by this class. The upper class reproduces itself through a myriad of social and cultural interlocking networks. One noted social scientist writes:

> There is a social upper class in the United States that is a ruling class by virtue of its dominant role in the economy and government. . . . [T]his ruling class is socially cohesive, has its basis in the large corporations and banks, plays a major role in shaping the social and political climate, and dominates the federal government through a variety of organizations and methods. (Domhoff, 1983, p. 1)

Class theorists argue that members of the upper class disproportionately hold the top leadership roles in America. Class researchers such as William Domhoff acknowledge the incorporation of formerly marginal groups (e.g., Jews) into the upper class, yet argue that membership in the upper economic class is the primary route to power within business, culture, and government.

One neo-Marxist variation of the upper-class thesis argues that such economic determinism is overstated and that social sectors have some autonomy. This perspective (which could be labeled neo-Gramscian) explicitly rejects the notion that the capitalist class directly and overtly rules through the coercive power of the state. Maintaining the social order is not accomplished simply through the blatant use or threat of force. Instead, class rule exists because the cultural, political, ethical, and intellectual elite articulates a worldview that everyone, ruling and ruled, comes to uphold. Adoption of the supporting worldview occurs through its embodiment in social processes, organizations, and institutions. Given the assumption of ongoing class struggle, the dominant class constantly seeks new vehicles by which it can offset the revolutionary impulses of the working class; in colloquial parlance, it looks for new and better ways to maintain the workers' "false consciousness." This neo-Marxist view, then, defines the critical issue as not who owns capital, but who runs the institutions that further the domination of the capitalist class.

The alternative view of social structure and social influence derives from a non-Marxist framework, drawing heavily from the writings of Max Weber and Emile Durkheim on the structure of society. In this view, elites, not an upper class, hold power, by virtue of their positions at the very top of critical societal sectors. While elite theorists are divided with regard to whether American leadership consists of a singular American elite or multiple elites, they reject the notion of class dominance.

The Classics: Mosca, Pareto, and Michels

Since Aristotle political scientists have asked, "Who rules?" For the most part, rulers have been few, and the ruled have been many.[1] In eighteenth-century Europe, however, some intellectuals demanded direct, populist democracy: all men, created equal, should have an equal share in power. The democratic revolution sweeping Western Europe culminated in Marx's condemnation of bourgeois capitalism, his Communist-utopian dream of a workers' revolution, and his belief in the inevitable withering away of the state.

The classical elite theorists—Mosca, Pareto, and Michels—wrote in reaction to the rising tide of socialism and social democracy. They self-consciously set out to describe political behavior as it was, not as it ought to be. Each claimed that every society in reality was ruled by the few, not the many. Even supposed "democracies" proved to be no exception. Pareto makes the point most eloquently:

> Let us suppose that in every branch of human activity an index or grade can be assigned to each individual as an indication of his capacity. To the man who has earned millions—no matter what means he has employed therein, fair or foul—we will . . . give 10. To the earner of thousands we will give 6, assigning 1 to the man who just manages to keep body and soul together, and zero to him who ends up in the work house. . . . Let us therefore make a class for those people who have the highest indices in their branch of activity and give to this class the name of *elite*. . . .[W]e distinguish two further classes within this main class of the elite: the governing elite and the non-governing elite. The first elite class includes those who directly or indirectly play a significant part in government and political life; the second comprises the rest of the elite personnel, those who have no significant role in government and politics. (1966, p. 248)

Pareto goes on to develop a thesis of the ruling elite based on a division of personal leadership traits. He divides these into Class I residues, "the instinct of combinations," and Class II residues, "the institution of the persistence of aggregates" (see Parry, 1969, pp. 45–50; Parsons, 1968, pp. 178–300, esp. pp. 278–293; Aron, 1979, pp. 175–87).

Geraint Parry points out a parallel between Pareto's Class I and Class II personalities, and Machiavelli's foxes versus lions: Leaders are either intelligent and cunning (foxes), or brave, strong, and of good character (lions). The governing elite of the Class I type operate in the realm of words, ideologies, and political imagination. They disdain the use of force. Those of the Class II type use force, eliminating the opposition. Elites of the Class II type manifest many of the traits of the masses, who are also of Class II type, desiring political order above all. As with Machiavelli, Pareto contended a governing elite that balanced Class I and Class II traits was ideal.

Mosca used the term *political class* to describe the group that actually holds power in society. The political class, according to Mosca, is an organized minority of people who rule. He claimed that even in a democracy, only a few actually exercise significant power. Furthermore, members of the political class are not chosen at random. Recruitment into the political class is orderly, based on informal and formal rules. Over time, the criteria for ruling becomes more complex and differentiated, Mosca argued, because society has become more complex. In the past, elite rule was organized on the basis of religion, clan structure, or tradition. Modern societies demand specialized criteria for membership in the military elite, a different set of specialized rules to become part of the judiciary, and yet another set of conditions and rules to join the administrative bureaucracy.

Mosca clearly believed that the nature of contemporary elite rule is a function of the needs of modern society. Moreover, he claimed, elite recruitment from the middle stratum of society insures a system viability. Career mobility co-opts new members so that the ruling class retains its ties to the rest of society. Regardless of how open the ruling class may be, Mosca still believed that power could not rest with the populace.

Robert Michels developed his "iron law of oligarchy" after becoming disillusioned with mass politics and the possibility of a socialist revolution. He argued that the structure of modern society results in organization, which in turn means elite rule: "Who says organization, says oligarchy" (1958, p. 418). Michels examined the European socialist parties, especially the German Social Democratic Party, which claimed to be completely democratic. He found that to become powerful (i.e., to win elections), parties required specialization, a division of labor, and hierarchical organization. No matter how idealistic and oriented toward egalitarianism the founders of mass movements are, these organizations eventually and inevitably become oligarchic. The leaders in control of the party attempt to increase and perpetuate their power, an effort that requires both bureaucratic hierarchical organization and leadership. This is the iron law of oligarchy.

THE MODERN DEBATE: THE POWER ELITE VERSUS PLURAL ELITES

The twentieth-century debate on power in America has expanded conceptually. While the class-versus-elite dispute continues, a further wrinkle has been added to the intellectual debate among elite theorists. Is there one power elite, or are there many elites? The most famous work of the power elite school is C. Wright Mills's *The Power Elite*. Mills, like Mosca and Michels, defines the American elite in terms of their top positions in the most powerful institutions in America, not their role as representatives of the capitalist class. He sees American power as a ruling triumvirate of big government, big business, and the military.

> The power elite is composed of men whose positions enable them to transcend the ordinary environments of ordinary men and women; they are in positions to make decisions having major consequences. . . . [T]hey are in command of the major hierarchies and organizations of modern society. They rule the big corporations. They run the machinery of the state and claim its prerogatives. They direct the military establishment. They occupy the strategic command posts of the social structure, in which are now centered the effective means of the power and the wealth and the celebrity which they enjoy. (1956, pp. 3–4)

Subsequent theorists of the power elite school follow Mills and continue to argue that all power is fundamentally divided between two groups, the elite and the mass. The elite are homogeneous, cohesive, and autonomous, and represent the most exclusive segments of society. They seek to maximize their own power as opposed to mass interests. Political scientist James Meisel cleverly summarizes the features of a power elite: "group consciousness, coherence, and conspiracy" (meaning common goals and intentions, not secret societies; see Meisel, 1962, p. 4).

Political scientist Thomas Dye can also be classified as a power elite theorist. His textbook on who runs America characterizes American elites as "an oligarchic model of national policy making," which is a variation of the power elite model of American elites, although he does not think the elite to be secretive and conspiratorial. He does find a high degree of specialization among leaders of America's institutions such as corporate business, government, universities, philanthropic foundations, the media, and the military (1986, pp. 164–65).

At the same time, Dye argues, there is an inner group among these institutional leaders, which he calls "an elite within the elite" (pp. 156–69). These are leaders who hold positions across sectors and play "a major role in linking the corporate world with government, foundations, universities, cultural organizations, and civic associations" (p. 168). Dye views American elites ultimately as a single group along the lines of a power elite framework, although not as closed, interconnected, and secretive as Mills's business-government-military triumvirate.

Like Pareto, Dye finds a circulation of elites. There are multiple societal paths to the top, and Dye, like many other elite theorists, believes that openings at the top to a few of those below is necessary for society to maintain its vitality and stability. Nevertheless, he argues, leadership positions favor candidates from the upper class, as well as those who are white, male, and Protestant (pp. 185–218).

Dye further contends that *all* American leadership groups share certain fundamental values, such as "private property, limited government, separation of church and state, individual liberty, equality of opportunity, advancement based on merit, and due process of law" (p. 220). The conflicts within and among American elites stem from differences over specific policy questions (pp. 219–20). The question raised by power elite arguments, however, is strictly an empirical one: Is entry into the power elite primarily based on ascriptive criteria, that is, criteria that are strictly accidents of birth?

In opposition to the power elite theorists are the pluralists. They start from the premise of multiple and varying groups of elites. Pluralists believe that power in modern bureaucratic society reflects the structural conflicts of that society. Modern society contains a complex network of elite groups with varying agendas which sometimes cooperate with each other and sometimes battle each other. For the pluralists, power is diffuse, specialized, and differentiated. Unlike the power elite model, elites in a pluralist paradigm are multiple and fragmented.

Who Governs, by political scientist Robert Dahl, is often cited as the pluralist rejoinder to Mills's *The Power Elite.* Dahl's major objective was not to answer Mills. Rather he argued that America is a democracy (more precisely a "polyarchy"), even though most persons are not politically active. Dahl argues that humans are not political animals, but civic animals.

> The chances are very great that political activism will always seem rather remote from the main focus of his life. . . . Political action will seem considerably less efficient than working at his job, earning more money, taking out insurance, joining a club, planning a vacation, moving to another neighborhood or city, or coping with an uncertain future in manifold other ways. (1961, p. 224)

Most people, most of the time, are simply not interested in politics. Political participation in modern democratic society is not constant, but depends on the issue at stake. Participation is always a matter of interest. When civic people's interest is truly at stake, they will become politically active.

Dahl found that political involvement varied even among the three most prestigious groups in New Haven—the social notables, the eco-

nomic notables, and the political notables. Those with high social stand-
ing in the community were the least active among notables in general,
while economic notables were active on economic issues, but were not
involved in such issues as education. The elected politicians were, of
course, the most politically active, and were such over the largest range
of issues. Implicit in Dahl's analysis is the argument that varying degrees
of political activism among notables mean that those at the top are not a
power elite; to paraphrase Meisel (1962, p. 4), they are not self-con-
scious, cohesive, or self-contained.

Sociologists such as Arnold Rose and Suzanne Keller have also criticized the notion of a ruling class or a power elite; Keller's *Beyond the
Ruling Class: Strategic Elites in Modern Society* (1991, orig. 1963) provides the basis of our paradigm. Rose took Mills's *the Power Elite* as his
point of departure, refuting Mills's major point that power is concentrated in the hands of a select elite core. He observes that in every
organization, "every organized activity of American life and at every
level—national, regional, state, and local"—power is concentrated in
the hands of a few (1967, p. 484). Nevertheless, the multiple levels and
multiple spheres of power mean that no single national group exercises
control over all or even most issues. "Even in government and in actively
democratic trade unions, there is an ever-changing elite which exercises
most of the power at any given moment" (p. 485). Rose, like Dahl, finds
that each elite is powerful within its own sphere, but not in others,
although he recognizes that political and business leaders each exercise
considerable influence in the other's sphere. Thus governmental elites
involve themselves in economic policy, while businesses lobby politicians to influence public policy. Rose argues, however, that business
elites are the most effective lobbyists of government not merely because
they have the most money, but "because they are more educated, more
knowledgeable, more articulate, and more activist than average citizens"
(p. 485). In addition, Rose discusses the rise of local, state, regional, and
national voluntary associations, such as the National Association for the
Advancement of Colored People and the American Civil Liberties Union,
charity groups such as the Red Cross, and various religious groups.
These groups are organized around a common purpose, and participation and membership are voluntary. Groups of elites also emerge from
these numerous associations (pp. 244–52).

Rose neatly sums up the pluralists' critique of the ruling class view of
politics:

Mills has implicitly compared the existing American power structure
to some populist or guild socialist ideal, which has never existed and

to which we believe could never exist considering basic sociological facts. . . . We do not say that the multi-influence hypothesis is entirely the fact, or that the United States is completely democratic; we simply say that such statements are more correct for the United States today than for any other society. (p. 492).

In the next section, we examine in greater detail the issue of power versus plural elites in the context of our view of American social structure. For this discussion, we rely on Daniel Bell's *The Cultural Contradictions of Capitalism* (1978) and Keller's *Beyond the Ruling Class*.

IDENTIFYING AMERICAN ELITES

During the 1992 presidential election, Vice-President Dan Quayle raised the issue of the cultural elite and American values. Mentioned among the cultural elite was New York governor Mario Cuomo, who became quite indignant at being included in this group. Cuomo declared that he was not a member of the cultural elite, because he did not go to Harvard; he went to St. John's. What is wrong with these opposing formulations? Clearly, Cuomo equates elite membership status with upper-class status, while Quayle considers Cuomo's celebrity prominence as sufficient to include him in the cultural elite.

What is an elite, and what is the relationship, if any, between elite status and membership in the upper class? This chapter defines American elites in terms of the structure of modern American society and discusses the various types of elites: economic, governmental, and cultural. Defining our sample of American elites is clearly rooted in our underlying view of the critical sectors in modern industrial society. Like most social scientists, we start with the premise that modern society has become more complex, specialized, and differentiated. New occupational and technological sectors emerge, such as the computer and related industries of Silicon Valley. Accompanying them are new lifestyles and new "bedroom" communities, where minimal interaction takes place because residents have little in common except neighborhood.

Daniel Bell points out that the complexity of modern society has led to a disjunction of realms. He argues that during the Christian Middle Ages and at the dawn of liberal capitalism, social structure and culture were better integrated:

> Religion and its idea of hierarchy were reflected in the social structure of the feudal worlds, and religious passions infused the symbolism of the time. With the rise of the bourgeoisie, there may have been

a single societal mode threaded through all realms from economic relations to moral conduct to cultural conceptions to character structure. And at the time one could see history as a progressive advance in man's power over nature and himself. (1978, p. 10)

Bell characterizes the modern era, however, by its three distinct realms, each governed by different norms and habits, some in obvious conflict with each other: "Society, I would say, is not integral, but disjunctive, the different realms respond to different norms, have different rhythms of change, and are regulated by different, even contrary, axial principles" (p. 10).

The disjunction of spheres means that elites within spheres are also distinct, nonintegrated groups. American elites may grow in number, variety, and power, but they are far from a tight, interlocking, integrated network. Bell's view of social dislocation fits with Keller's definition of strategic elites. She argues that strategic elites, characterized as noncohesive, autonomous, and occupationally distinct, are an inevitable outcome of modern society.

In *Beyond the Ruling Class,* Keller contends that "strategic elites," not an upper class, characterize modern society. She defines strategic elites as those roles in society that have the responsibility for maintaining an institution, its roles, and its norms (pp. 4–6):

The term "elites" refers first of all to a minority of individuals designated to serve a collectivity in a socially valued way. Elites are effective and responsible minorities—effective as regards the performance of activities of interest and concern to others to whom these elites are responsive. Socially significant elites are ultimately responsible for the realization of major social goals and for the continuity of the social order. Continuity, as used here, implies contributing to an ongoing social process, and while not synonymous with survival includes the possibility of decline. (p. 4)

Drawing heavily from Emile Durkheim's analysis of the division of labor in modern society, Keller cites four main reasons why we see a proliferation of strategic elites: the growth of population, the growth of occupational specialization, the growth of formal organization (bureaucracy), and the growth of moral diversity (p. 65). Modern societies are highly populated. The Greek city-state numbered no more than twenty thousand. Its very size made possible direct democracy, extensive participation, and public spiritedness. Population growth has resulted in communities larger than twenty-thousand; with size has come increased occupational diversity. "In a smaller and occupationally less differentiated community," according to Keller, "all members must contribute toward its and their own survival. It tends to resemble a collective of like elements" (p. 67).

Larger and more inclusive societies, however, come with a more complex division of labor. In turn, society's leaders, its elite, become more differentiated and diverse. "The consequences [of greater differentiation] are the greater autonomy and independence of these elites, their smaller degree of cohesion, and the decreasing likelihood that any single elite can long exert absolute, arbitrary power" (p. 70).

Keller further argues that the notion of a single unified elite controlling modern society is simply a myth. Elites in modern society are occupationally distinct and too diverse to act in concert. Criteria for leadership have gradually changed over time to reflect this elite diversity. "Nobility of blood was displaced by nobility of wealth, and the latter now appears to be making way for a nobility of expert skill and interests" (p. 70).

With the growing diversity of occupations, and thus the growing diversity of elites, Keller argues, comes a growing moral diversity. "Nostalgia for the small, intimate, familiar community has increased in proportion to its decline. . . . Many of the moral ideals of today, the standards of right and wrong, sacred and profane, were developed in these simpler communities and continue to be taught alongside the mores better adapted to an urban way of life" (p. 74). She believes that strategic elites are the only groups in society that can give it any moral cohesion. "Individuals, though they still belong to the same society, no longer share all of its burdens and therefore cannot, except in the most abstract sense, live up to all of its ultimate moral claims. Today, only the strategic elites can do so" (p. 75).

Keller goes on to argue that strategic elites provide the moral ties that bind a modern society together. She believes that elites must provide this for modern society to function smoothly.

> In this sense, strategic elites resemble communities—they must feel committed to larger collective purposes within a common cultural framework. Most people in their everyday working lives, tend to refer to "they," the anonymous eyes and ears of the world or the men in control of things as sources of authority. The strategic elites, who are the originators rather than the instruments of social action, must be able, at least some of the time, to say "we." (p. 76)

This view is as much a hope as a reality. By implication, Bell's argument (1978) that American life is divided into disjointed spheres suggests that elites in general lack moral cohesion. Value cohesion exists within spheres, but not between them. In fact, his work suggests a significant degree of antagonism between the cultural realm and the economic-technological realm.

One of the propositions we can draw from the writings of Bell (1978) and Keller (1991) is that modern American elites are defined primarily by their occupational positions. If the critical sectors of American society are disjointed, these elites will have little in common. The lack of commonality starts with social background and includes a wide array of attitudes and general ways of looking at the world, rather than a common moral framework.

Elites may be located in one of three sectors: the economy, the polity, or the culture; these sectors parallel Bell's description of modern American society as consisting of three disjunctive spheres: the culture, the polity, and the technoeconomic structure.

Elites of the Economic Sector

In the economic sector, the heads of large corporations are part of the American elite, but the economic sector has also changed considerably during the past 70 years in two significant ways. One is the transformation of business into the modern corporation; the other is the post–New Deal federal regulation of business.

In the modern corporate bureaucracy, many businesses such as the Ford Motor Company have passed from the hands of the original founder to control by company executives, boards of trustees, and a larger group of stockholders. This transition is also evident in the newer computer industries, where the original creators of the Apple Computer have nothing to do with the current company.

This change of the modern corporation has created what James Burnham (1942) called the new managerial elite, often "credentialized" in recent years by the masters degree in business administration (although its popularity has dropped off significantly since the late 1970s and early 1980s).

A survey of the business elite was completed by Rothman and Lichter in 1979. Upper and middle management personnel were randomly drawn from the official company lists of four Fortune 500 companies and of one firm in each category of *Fortune* lists of the fifty leading retail outlets, banks, and public utilities (Rothman and Lichter, 1984).[2]

Complementing our sample of the business elite are the leaders of America's largest unions. With government regulation of the economy, labor unions have become more than a workers' group reacting to man-agement. Labor's role has expanded beyond opposition to corporation policies, and trade union leaders currently play a significant role in shaping American trade and economic policy, despite the decline in trade union strength during the past twenty-five years. Moreover, they are perceived to be closely aligned with the national Democratic party. Inso-far as we have a national and international economy, and given that government regulates the marketplace, labor leaders form a national elite. Rothman and Lichter sampled the leaders of national labor unions and trade associations as well as the heads of major locals in 1984 and 1985.

Elite members of the corporate bar are also included in this study. Corporate law is a critical profession in the modern capitalist economy because of the rise of the modern rational-legal organization. In 1982, Rothman and Lichter sampled the corporate legal elite, defined as part-ners in major corporate law firms in Washington, DC, and New York.

Political Elites

The fundamental roles of the polity are the determination of which social values are to be maximized, how values are to be distributed among the populace, and how conflict is to be managed. Political elites (by which we mean more than just politicians) define what is and is not private versus public, fair, just, and legal. This sphere ranges from dis-putes of everyday public life, in which the local police break up a fight on the street, through conflicts between nations. With the expansion of the national government, political elites have increased in kind and number. In addition, elite groups in other sectors—for example, business and labor, the media elite, and elite academics—play a significant role in shaping the federal agenda through such activities as lobbying, consult-ing, and testifying. The scope of the national government and the na-tional (and international) impact of mass communications means that most national elites play some kind of political role. For the sake of describing the elites surveyed for this study, we have limited political elites to include those elites whose primary mission revolves around government. Many political scientists have studied presidents and mem-bers of Congress as part of the national elite. Rothman and Lichter surveyed other political elites, including military leaders, federal civil servants, congressional aides, federal judges, and public interest group leaders.

THE MILITARY ELITE. Despite President Eisenhower's farewell address warning of the power of a "military industrial complex" (quoted in Keller, 1991, p. 285), the United States has increasingly relied on a professional military. Moreover, one noted sociologist makes the point that the administration and organization of the military increasingly resembles that of a business corporation: "The professional soldier is required more and more to acquire skills and orientations common to civilian administrators and even political leaders" (Morris Janowitz, quoted in Keller, 1991, p. 285).

Keller points out, however, that the mission of the military remains distinctive. No other group is legally given the authority to protect and defend the nation, despite the military's organizational similarity with other legal-rational structures in the civil service and private corporations. Moreover, "the military elite must be prepared to kill and to die—a fate that is uniquely its own" (p. 286). As a result, the military has developed a number of strongly ingrained traditions and norms, some of which conflict with civilian life patterns. Its unique role has sometimes enabled the military to retain its way of doing things despite changes in the larger society.[3] The military elite that were surveyed by Rothman and Lichter in 1982 are a random sample of high-ranking officers (see the appendix for details).

THE FEDERAL CIVIL SERVICE. With the expansion of the executive branch, the size and power of the federal civil service have increased. Bureaucrats now play an important role in setting the national political agenda. Rothman and Lichter surveyed senior civil service executives, covering both the newer, activist agencies as well as those in more traditional bureaus and departments. Half the sample came from agencies such as the Justice Department's Civil Rights Division, the Environmental Protection Agency, the Federal Trade Commission, and the Department of Health and Human Services. The other half of senior civil servants were from "traditional" agencies, such as the departments of Commerce and Agriculture and the Internal Revenue Service, among others.

CONGRESSIONAL AIDES. Expansion of federal power has meant a larger role for the legislative branch. Congressional staff play a critical part in helping individual members of Congress deal with the volumes of legislation that pass their desks daily. This is necessary because members of congress are generalists; their aids develop the necessary technical expertise to understand and assist in crafting the details of complex legislation. In the process, congressional aides directly influence policy. In 1982, Rothman and Lichter drew a random sample of congressional aides from key committee and personal staff.

FEDERAL JUDGES.   In *Democracy in America,* Tocqueville notes that political questions in America often are transformed into judicial questions. Like other branches of national government, the judiciary has grown in size and influence. Activist judges have intervened in many controversial issues such as prisoners' rights, school desegregation, and most recently, gays and lesbians in the military. Rothman and Lichter surveyed a random sample of federal judges in 1982. An equal number were drawn from both the appellate and the district levels in selected circuits.

THE PUBLIC INTEREST ELITE.   Unlike other elite groups, the public interest elite are formally outside government. These organizations represent people they claim lie outside the traditional political arena. These groups are supposedly unorganized and thus lack the interest-group clout of business and labor, who constantly lobby the states and the national government. The public interest movement represents what some conservatives call "victim" groups (e.g., blacks, women, children, Hispanics, consumers) and the environment. Rothman and Lichter surveyed the leaders of important public interest groups in 1982.

The Cultural Elite

Cultural elites are involved in the creation and distribution of symbols. The pervasiveness of television, film, and the news media has nationalized the cultural elite and changed its nature. Cultural elites deal with issues that, in Bell's words,

> confront all human beings, through all times, in the nature of consciousness: how one meets death, the nature of tragedy and the character of heroism, the definition of loyalty and obligation, the redemption of the soul, the meaning of love and of sacrifice, the understanding of compassion, the tension between an animal and a human nature, the claims of instinct and restraint. (1978, p. 12)

How particular cultural institutions deal with these issues varies widely. Religion meets Bell's definition of significant institutions in the cultural sphere. High-brow, mid-brow, and low-brow cultures address these questions in the secular realm, using different means. Presumably, classical and modern art and classical music are high-brow, insofar as their appeal is limited to those few trained to appreciate these forms. Low-brow culture is mass culture, seeking to appeal to the many, and mid-brow cultures seeks to blend the values of high-brow and the vehicles of mass culture—for example, television, and the movies. To capture the views of the cultural elite, Rothman and Lichter sampled elite members of the news media, film, and television industries; they also sampled American religious leaders.

THE MEDIA ELITE.   The rise of mass communications and mass technology has been instrumental in creating a national political community. Regional and class boundaries eroded with the rise of the motion picture industry, newspaper chains, and national weekly magazines such as *Time* and *Newsweek*. Television further accelerated societywide integration. These developments have led to an interesting paradox. Rothman notes how such integration of mass communication "increased the influence of a few eastern media outlets. . . . With sources of political news increasingly centered in New York and Washington . . . key newspapers and magazines on the east coast took on new importance" (Rothman, 1992a, p. 47).

Focusing on national media outlets, Rothman and Lichter defined the media elite as including journalists and editors from the *New York Times, Washington Post, Wall Street Journal, Time, Newsweek, U.S. News and World Report,* and the news organizations at NBC, ABC, CBS, and PBS. Given their emphasis on national institutions, the researchers excluded regional and local newspapers.[4]

THE FILMMAKERS.   As Powers, Rothman, and Rothman (1992) note, the creators of successful movies reach many people very quickly; their range is exceeded only by the makers of prime-time television. Moreover, the number of persons directly involved in shaping the content of the movies is relatively small. "Although most movies, particularly those that Hollywood produces, have always been group efforts, the numbers of creative workers are relatively small, an elite group who work together over and over" (p. 268). Powers and colleagues further note that the post–World War II decline of studio control, in combination with the rise of independent producers and talent agencies, enabled the creative movie elite to produce films that closely express their own values. "Younger, better educated, and more cosmopolitan, these new members of the Hollywood elite brought with them certain attitudes and orientations that were quite different from those several generations preceding them" (p. 269). For this study of American leadership groups, Rothman and Lichter surveyed ninety-six producers, writers, and directors, randomly sampled from a list of the most popular movies made between 1960 and 1982.

THE MAKERS OF PRIME-TIME TELEVISION.   The newest contributors to nationalizing American life are the creators of prime-time television. Along with movies and the news media, prime-time television breaks down regional, ethnic, and class barriers. It both shapes and reflects societal norms and mores. Liberal and conservative critics alike decry the impact of television entertainment with regard to sex and violence, but also its tendency to erode standards of civility.

Rothman and Lichter randomly sampled 104 creators of prime-time television in 1982, including the writers, producers, and executives associated with developing at least two successful prime-time television series.

AMERICAN RELIGIOUS ELITE.   American religious life is composed of three distinct, albeit related, types. The first is highly individualistic and focuses on salvation through personal belief. Even in the Puritan colonies, personal salvation preceded membership in a church (Bellah et al., 1985, p. 233).

The second American religious tradition is rooted in the formation of local congregations and, combined with American religious individualism, produces a religious pluralism unique to the United States.

The third religious tradition is what Bellah and colleagues call the "religious center," which melds the mainline Protestant churches, the Catholic church, and the evangelical denominations into a center of American culture by emphasizing a commonality of traditions (pp. 237–39):

> Today there are not only denominational bureaucracies and clerical hierarchies, a wide variety of educational and charitable religious institutions, and numerous religious organizations oriented to social and political action, but also religious intellectuals who command the attention of segments of the general public, not to mention media stars of the electronic churches. However private religion may be at the levels of the individual and the local church, at this third, or cultural, level religion is part of public life, even though the way in which it is public and the appropriate content of its public message are subject to controversy. (pp. 226–27)

Rothman and Lichter defined the American religious elite as the leaders of major Christian denominations, the leading figures of religious social action groups, the editors of religious journals, and prominent theologians. These groups were surveyed in 1984 and 1985.

Our description of the twelve groups analyzed for this study by no means includes all strategic elites; however, it is the most complete picture thus far. We did not include academic elites because we felt that Ladd and Lipset (1975) had effectively dealt with them. We incorporated some of the findings of another study of ours (Nagai, Lerner, and Rothman, 1994), which looks at leaders of major philanthropic foundations. The ideal study would include the president, his cabinet, the Supreme Court, Congress, governors, and the mayors of large cities, but these individuals and groups are not part of this study.

Mario Cuomo was partly right. He was not a member of the cultural elite at the time he made the statement. He was governor of New York. His job had inherently little to do with shaping the value orientation and worldview of the American public, which is our definition of the role of cultural elites. However, Cuomo was also partly wrong. Membership in the American political elite has little to do with where one went to college. The fact that he was governor of New York made him a member of the political elite.

The next chapter takes the Cuomo criticism of Quayle's statement more seriously. Is it necessary to be born into a wealthy family and to attend a prestigious school to become part of the American elite? Perhaps Mario Cuomo's humble roots are the exception, not the rule. In the next chapter we turn to some survey results, examining the socio-demographic background of American elites and general patterns of elite mobility.

ROOM AT THE TOP: ISSUES OF SOCIAL CLASS, EDUCATION, AND ACCESS TO POWER

Americans are ambivalent about those at the top. We admire individuals who get ahead because they work hard and perform well. We therefore believe that government should insure an equality of opportunity. At the same time, many believe that America should place greater emphasis on an equality of outcomes. The argument is that if we were truly a meritocratic society, then every person would have an equal chance of reaching the top. If this were the case, elites would resemble a random sample of the general population, differing only in terms of individual effort and skill. Thus, half of elites would be women, 12 percent would be African American, roughly 3 percent would be Jewish, and so on. We acknowledge that racism, sexism, and other forms of societal discrimination, in addition to the more general processes of societal stratification, produce an inequality of results.

Much of the debate regarding social mobility in America centers around what criteria lie beneath the American system of stratification. Are certain conditions necessary or merely sufficient for reaching the top? Moreover, do they vary by occupation?

The issues can be summarized in terms of the importance of achievement versus ascription among American elites. Achieved characteristics result from what individuals accomplish through their own efforts. For example, a doctoral degree is an achieved characteristic, since it requires considerable effort on the part of the individual to earn a Ph.D.; the degree cannot be inherited from one's parents. Similarly, most occupations, especially those requiring professional accreditation (a law or medical degree), cannot be handed down directly through generations as one would a trust fund.

Nevertheless, some occupational (elite) achievements are helped along by ascriptive characteristics, which are circumstances that cannot be changed through individual effort. They are, in effect, accidents of birth. The son of Henry Ford enters the world with social and material resources unavailable to the son of a day laborer.

The society of truly equal opportunity, where every person has an equal chance of becoming a member of the ruling elite, is the perfect but nonexistent society. Such a society would look like Plato's *Republic*, where children are taken away from their birth parents to be raised by the city. Those with the souls of the guardian class, regardless of their parentage, would be educated to rule.

In the case of the American elite, various ascriptive and achieved traits are relevant. We look first at education, which is usually taken to be an indicator of achieved status. Putnam (1976, p. 52) observes how every system has numerous techniques for separating people desiring positions of power from those who actually have positions of power. These rules of selection serve as norms guiding mobility and routinizing the process of recruitment. In other words, these standards act as gatekeepers in the maintenance of elites.

Keller (1991) argues that in a system such as the American one people with power are strategic elites, presiding over sectors of the society (the economy, the polity, and the culture). This means that levels of education and professional certification (e.g., a law degree) serve as one type of gatekeeping or filtering device regulating admission into the American elite.

EDUCATION. As a group, the American elite are well-educated (see Table 2.1). We find that elites in occupations that are highly bureaucratized have the highest and most uniform levels of education. Ninety percent of the American elite have graduated from college, compared with only 19 percent of the American public.[1] Leaders of the labor movement are the only elite group in which less than a majority are college graduates. Not surprisingly, all those in occupations requiring professional certification (civil service, law, the military) are college graduates.

One in ten businessmen and women lack college degrees, a finding that can be interpreted in two ways. The world of corporate business may still rely somewhat more on individual effort and on-the-job perfor-

TABLE 2.1 Social Background of American Elites

	Male	Mean Age		White	English	Jewish	College Degree	Elite College[a]	N
		Men	Women						
Bureaucrats	93	49	48	93	23	21	98	24	200
Business	93	46	35	97	22	8	89	25	242
Congressional aides	73	36	33	94	28	10	95	24	134
Judges	95	61	53	89	32	18	99	47	114
Labor	97	55	45	95	29	13	38	6	95
Lawyers	98	48	48	99	29	40	100	68	150
Media	79	44	35	95	24	26	95	37	238
Military	99	48	43	95	27	1	100	24	152
Movies	99	49	60	99	12	56	63	28	96
Public interest	69	41	34	97	25	48	100	45	158
Religious leaders	85	54	49	87	26	0	98	19	178
Television	92	49	39	99	21	58	75	22	104

[a]"Highly selective undergraduate institutions," as defined and ranked by Ladd and Lipset in their study of university and college professors (1975).

mance than on college degrees. Another interpretation is that at least some members of the business elite are promoted on the basis of personal and social ties rather than educational achievement.

Most occupations involved in the production of culture are not bureaucratic, nor do they demand professional certification. Exceptions are the professorate (which we did not study), religious leaders, and to a lesser extent the news media.

College graduates also dominate the industries of prime-time television and popular movies, although in significantly smaller proportions than in such professions as law and the military.[2] A surprisingly large proportion of the cultural elite, however, has graduated from America's most selective institutions of higher learning.[3] Twenty-two percent of the makers of prime-time television, 28 percent of America's leading filmmakers, and 37 percent of the news media elite come from elite colleges and universities. This is roughly equal to or greater than the percentage of business leaders and federal bureaucrats who have graduated from elite institutions.

Higher education, especially elite-school education, is clearly an asset in attaining elite status. In almost all cases, a college degree is a highly desirable condition, although only necessary in occupations requiring professional certification. The advantages of a college degree are apparent even among the newer, nonbureaucratic occupations such as prime-time television and film. Since a college degree is an achieved not ascribed characteristic, elite status is, to some extent, achieved.

Ascribed characteristics (sex, race, ethnicity, and social class) limit access to the top stratum of society. It is not equally open to bright and ambitious individuals, no matter what their circumstances of birth.

Social Background and Social Mobility Among American Elites

As noted earlier, the more a society favors ascription over achievement, the more it resembles a system of upper-class rule. In such systems, authority is narrowly limited to a few in a single status, the upper class. Moreover, the scope of upper-class rule is wide, compared with the scope of authority of strategic elites, which is narrowly limited to their particular occupations (Keller, 1991, p. 58).

Noted sociologist Digby Baltzell (1979, pp. 24–26) contrasts elite and upper-class rule. Like Keller, he defines elites as "those individuals in any social system who hold the top positions in their chosen careers, occupations, or professions" (p. 24). Thomas Jefferson, Baltzell notes, referred to them as a "natural aristocracy" in free democracies. The problem is that the descendants of the natural aristocrats become a hereditary upper class. "An upper class," Baltzell observes,

> is a *sociological* and *historical,* rather than *natural* aristocracy; it is nothing more or less than *a group of consanguine familes* whose ancestors were elite members and family founders one or more generations earlier. Thus, Oliver Wendell Holmes, Jr., and John Winthrop IV were members of the New England upper class; John G. Johnson and David Rittenhouse were natural aristocrats and elite Philadelphians but neither founders nor sons of any upper-class family in the city. (p. 25)

> By the late nineteenth century, the American elite moved from a "natural aristocracy" to becoming a closed, privileged caste, marked by ethnic prejudice and "a debilitating Anglo-Saxonism." (p. 20)

Although most occupations and institutions today cannot legally discriminate on the basis of race, religion, or gender,[4] the debate continues as to the relative importance of ascription versus achievement (or upper-class versus natural aristocracy). The question now is to what extent and what kind of ascriptive features still assist some persons more than others.

It has become a cliché to say that American elites are predominantly white, Protestant men. They are far from representative of the general public on the traits of sex and race. These broadest of ascriptive traits are perhaps the last (but perhaps the hardest) ascriptive barriers to overcome. The "ruling class" stereotype of American elites fits primarily if we limit the stereotype to the broadest and most inclusive categories of gender, race, and class.

GENDER.   American elites are overwhelmingly male (see Table 2.1), and the percentages do not vary much by profession.[5] Men dominate even in the newest of elite professions, the public interest movement, although significantly less so when compared with other groups. In addition, women elites on average are significantly younger than the men (thirty-nine years versus forty-eight years old), suggesting that a few women may be the first beneficiaries of affirmative action and may be on a faster promotion track.

RACE.   As one would expect, American elites are overwhelmingly white. In 1983, 85 percent of the American public were white, 12 percent were African American (Statistical Abstract, 1985, p. 27). Among elites,

95 percent were white, 4 percent were African American, and 1 percent were of either Asian or Latino origin. Whites are disproportionately represented in almost all elite groups, except for religious leaders and the federal judiciary, where the percentage of whites and blacks comes closer to resembling the general public. Somewhat surprisingly, in light of the celebrated career of Gen. Colin Powell, whites are disproportionately found even among military leaders, where they make up 95 percent. While the American military is thought to be relatively more hospitable to blacks compared with other occupations, this may hold only for lower ranks; it was not the case for the military elite as of 1985.

ETHNICITY AND RELIGION.   The ethnic and religious composition of American elites is far from a bastion of the Anglo-Saxon Protestant establishment. This is true even for the older, more established occupations such as corporate business and law. Indeed, if we compare American elites with the general public, we find only a slightly higher proportion of Anglo-Saxon Protestants among the elite (Statistical Abstract, 1985, pp. 33, 35) and a greater proportion of Jews. Roughly one in four members of American elites are of British descent, compared with 21 percent of the general public; 23 percent of elites claim either Jewish ethnic or Jewish religious affiliation, compared with 2 percent of the general public (p. 52).

The percentage of Jewish elites raises a serious question about the underlying issues concerned with the "nonrepresentative" nature of American elites. The literature on elites, including our own studies, emphasizes the nonrepresentative nature of elites. The "maleness" and "whiteness" of American elites are used as evidence of a relatively closed system that discriminates, at the minimum, on the basis of the ascriptive characteristics of sex and race.

A purely open system would presumably result in a distribution of ascriptive characteristics that matched the traits of the general public. When one group is disproportionately represented, the argument is that that group is being singled out for special treatment. The argument of group representation fails, however, when a proportion of a group previously discriminated against emerges as significantly overrepresented in comparison with its numbers in the general population. This is the issue raised by the proportion of Jewish elites in our sample.

One might discount those occupations that have long been assumed to be disproportionately Jewish—film, television, and the news media. Similarly, however, we should discount those occupations such as the religious elite (which Rothman and Lichter defined by membership size,

thus excluding Jewish religious leaders) and the military (which traditionally has not been a popular occupation among American Jews).

How do Jewish and WASP elites fare in the traditional establishment
occupations—the federal government, corporate business, and corporate law? There are roughly the same proportion of WASPs and Jews at
the elite levels of the federal civil service, and a greater proportion of
Jewish elites among corporate lawyers. The only arena that seems to
retain its "establishment" stereotype is the corporate business world.
There, 22 percent are WASPs, while only 8 percent are Jewish. Given the
Jewish proportion of American population, however, Jews are overrepresented even in this sector.

CLASS BACKGROUND.   As Thomas Dye (1986, p. 192) notes, the issue of
class is "a touchy subject." He points out that most Americans tend to
think of themselves as "middle class," while members of the upper class
tend to hide their class. In addition, Dye points out that analysis of elites
"must avoid the circularity of saying 'the power elite is the upper class'
and then defining the upper class as 'the power elite'" (p. 193).

Dye suggests that focusing on social origins of elites avoids the problem of circular reasoning. Is class origin, an ascriptive trait, a significant
factor in reaching the top? Dye's own research defines upper-class origins
in terms of several factors. First, did the person attend a prestigious
preparatory school? Second, was the parent's occupation one of the following: officer or director of a corporation, bank, insurance company,
utility; a high-ranking government or military official; partner in a major
law firm; owner of a newspaper; trustee or president of a major nonprofit
organization (e.g., university or philanthropic foundation)?

Dye finds that only 30 percent of the corporate, governmental, and
civic elite of American come from an upper-class background.[6] Seventy
percent of them are "middle class in family origin." He fails however, to
define middle-class origins except as involving parents who lacked high
institutional positions but whose children went to college (p. 194).

In Rothman and Lichter's surveys of American elites, respondents
were asked about their parents' (mostly fathers') jobs, their family income while growing up, and how much education their parents had.
Because the Rothman-Lichter questions differ somewhat from Dye's
analysis of elites' social background, we cannot make direct comparisons. We do not know what schools the respondents attended before
college, nor do we know which had fathers who were members of one
elite group or another.

We can, however, ask whether those of higher class background

(based on father's occupation, income, and education) are disproportionately found among American elites. Are there any who rose from the
blue-collar classes, or from the poor? (See Table 2.2.) Looking at the
fathers' education, we find considerable social mobility. Twenty-nine
percent of the total sample had fathers who never finished high school.
This includes more than one-third of those employed in traditional establishment occupations such as the civil service and business.

Compared with the general public, the American elite is still disproportionately drawn from middle- and upper-class backgrounds. Nevertheless, only 37 percent of all elites claim to have grown up in families
that were above average in family income. In contrast, 29 percent of
American elites say their families were below average. Table 2.2 shows
that even in traditional occupations such as business, the civil service,
and law, a significant proportion of elites grew up in relatively poor
circumstances.

Recollections of past family income are problematic, however, especially given Americans' reluctance to acknowledge coming from wealthy
families. To further examine social origins, we turned to the father's
occupation and categorized fathers' jobs using the Duncan Scale of Occupational Categories (Blau and Duncan, 1967). Using the aggregate
categories provided by Blau and Duncan, we then collapsed the scale into
the more common coding categories of upper-status white collar, lower-
status white collar, blue collar and farm labor, other, and none.

Most elites are the sons and daughters of upper-status white-collar
workers. Labor leaders come from blue-collar families, however, as do
many military and religious leaders. At the other extreme, a larger percentage of the media elite and public interest leaders than is true of any
other elite group grew up in high-status families (see Table 2.2).

Taken as a whole, public interest leaders are the most anomalous
group of elites. If one looks solely at social-class origins, they come from
the most advantaged social backgrounds. Their leaders are among the
best educated, come from the most elite schools, and have relatively well-
off, high-status white-collar, highly educated fathers. At the same time,
the public interest movement includes proportionately more women
leaders than other groups, as well as one of the largest proportion of Jews.

While the American elite draws some of its members from lower-
middle-class or working-class backgrounds, it was, at the time of this
study, disproportionately white, male, and of high-status origins. These
ascriptive traits, while not strictly speaking necessary, are helpful in
predicting success. How then may we best portray access to the American elite? Political scientist Robert Putnam (1976) illustrated four differ-

TABLE 2.2 Social Origins of American Elites

| | Grew Up[a] | | Father's Education | | Father's Socioeconomic Status | | |
	Poor	Well-off	No High School Degree	Graduate Degree	Blue Collar	Upper White Collar	N
Bureaucrats	31	34	36	14	31	47	196
Business	30	32	34	11	32	57	241
Congressional aides	13	43	17	23	27	50	132
Judges	23	47	23	27	20	59	103
Labor	52	15	65	1	65	22	94
Lawyers	20	56	22	35	16	68	148
Media	26	44	23	25	17	70	237
Military	35	29	32	12	36	36	152
Movies	31	40	29	9	26	49	90
Public interest	15	55	12	41	13	73	156
Religious leaders	41	22	40	15	31	43	174
Television	34	32	27	16	21	61	104

[a]Respondents were asked to recall what their family income was when they were growing up. In the table, categories are collapsed so that "well below average" and "below average" are labeled "poor," while "well above average" and "above average" are labeled "well-off."

Figure 2.1 Putnam's Four Models of Elite Mobility.

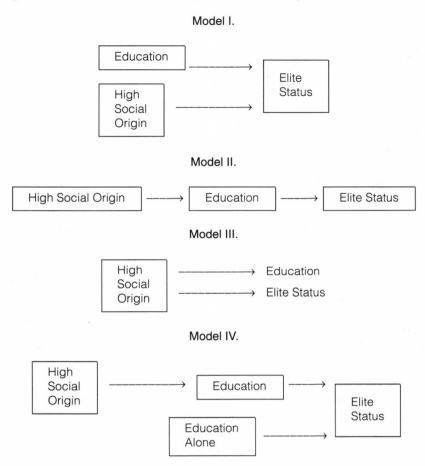

ent relationships between education and social origins. His models facilitate analysis of the relationship between achievement and ascription among American leadership groups (see Figure 2.1).

PUTNAM'S MODELS OF THE INTERACTION BETWEEN EDUCATION AND ASCRIPTIVE TRAITS.   The advantages that supposedly accrue on the basis of sex, race, religion, and social class are never clearly spelled out in actual application. Putnam (1976) contends that most studies fail to distinguish different routes to elite status. As an example, he looks at the relationships between high socioeconomic status, high educational attainment, and elite position.

Putnam notes how elite status based on educational credentials measures, for some, a society's emphasis of achievement over ascription. "Elite recruitment based on educational credentials is often seen as a means of breaking the pattern of . . . inheritance by which elites have traditionally bequeathed power to their children. When success rests on learned and testable skills rather than on inherited prerogatives, access to elite positions is presumably meritocratic" (p. 28).

Putnam goes on to point out, however, that we have to discuss the relationship between social class, an ascriptive trait, and access to education before concluding that greater emphasis on educational credentials means greater openness of the social system (p. 28). In Putnam's Model I, educational attainment and high socioeconomic status are both independent conditions for elite status. A member of an elite group can have either great educational credentials *or* the right social background. This enables individuals from lower classes to rise to the top without completely overhauling the existing social system.

In contrast, Model II is a system of no mobility. Educational attainment is a necessary desideratum of elite status, but one must be of higher status to get the necessary education. The diagram of Model II (p. 30) shows that one cannot get education without the proper social origins. Putnam's example (p. 29) is of the Chinese civil service. High social origins in China give the candidate tremendous advantages in passing the test, although social class cannot automatically assure one of passing, or make one an elite civil servant.

Putnam's example does not match his ideal type, because one could be of lower social origins and still become a civil servant by passing the exam, no matter how remote those chances might have been. The true manifestation of Model II is the Japanese civil service during the last years of Tokugawa Japan. There, as in China, applicants had to pass the traditional exam based on Confucian learning, but by and large, only those born of the samurai class were allowed by law to take the test; no farmers or merchants could apply (Koh, 1989).

Model III also exhibits a no-mobility option. High social status is a necessary (and sufficient) condition for elite positions. Educational attainment is irrelevant. Educational credentials, for those who have them, are merely an incidental by-product of higher class status.

Model IV is a variation of models II and III. Social background provides greater access to educational attainment for some members of the elite, but acquiring a proper educational background alone can also lead to elite positions. This model accounts for the disproportionate number of persons among the elite from upper-class status with college degrees.

At the same time, it does not restrict the entry of those of lower-class backgrounds, although there would be considerably fewer persons entering elite ranks as compared with Model I. In contrast to Model I societies, however, Model IV requires those of high social origins to have an education in order to acquire elite status.

The data show that Putnam's Model IV best explains the American pattern of achieving elite status. The socioeconomic indicators show that some advantages accrue to those born of higher socioeconomic status (SES) but that education, independent of class background, is an alternative means to reaching the top. Hardly any elite members from high-status backgrounds lack the educational requisites of elite status, indicating that such origins improve the chances of achieving elite status, but mediated through educational achievement. At the same time, achievement, as measured by educational attainment, has an independent effect. Some from lower-class families can obtain the requisite educational credentials necessary to make it to the top.

The impact of class on elite educational attainment is shown in Table 2.3. Almost all those elites raised in upper-status white-collar families (93 percent) but also lower-status white-collar families (92 percent) have college degrees. The gap occurs between blue-collar families and the others. Eighty-four percent of those from blue-collar families have college degrees. The percentage of college-educated elites from blue-collar families is sizable, but smaller than those raised in white-collar families.[7]

In our sample a higher SES provides more substantial opportunities for access to highly selective undergraduate education. According to Table 2.4, only 16 percent of college-educated elites from blue-collar homes went to the best schools. In contrast, roughly one in three college-

TABLE 2.3   Social Origin, Father's Income, and Education for Elite Samples

	Completed College or Better	N
Social origin		
Professional, managerial	93	962
Clerical, sales	92	280
Blue collar	84	483
Father's income		
Well above average	95	152
Above average	95	536
Average	89	616
Below average	87	398
Well below average	80	125

TABLE 2.4   Social Origin, Father's Income, and Access
to the Best Schools

	Respondent Attended Highly Selective Undergraduate School	N
Social origin		
Professional, managerial	39	962
Clerical, sales	34	280
Blue collar	16	483
Father's income		
Well above average	63	152
Above average	41	536
Average	25	616
Below average	19	398
Well below average	31	125

educated elites from low-status white-collar homes and almost four in ten college-educated members of the elite from upper-status white-collar families attended America's best colleges and universities. Correspondingly, almost two-thirds of those reporting substantially higher than average family incomes when they were growing up attended the best undergraduate institutions. In contrast, such schools were attended by fewer than one in three of those from the poorest homes and roughly two in five of those growing up in relatively comfortable homes.

Despite the prominence of the well-to-do at America's best schools, the social background of American elites is far from a tight-knit network of upper-class dominance, predominantly from America's best schools. The varied social background of American elites shows that they do not form an upper class. Many do not have "old school" ties, nor are they of Anglo-Saxon Protestant backgrounds. Many of their fathers were not upper-status white-collar professionals or managers, but lower-status white- and blue-collar workers, such as shopkeepers, salesmen, clerical workers, and laborers.

What are the implications of the lack of social commonality? Upper-class rule also means that the upper class forms "an endogamous subculture" (Baltzell, 1979, p. 32). Domhoff (1983, pp. 44–47) identifies upper-class members as those who are listed in the *Social Register,* attend exclusive boarding schools, or who belong to an exclusive social club. These social mechanisms serve to maintain an upper class because they inculcate an exclusive and distinctive upper-class subculture, possessing a distinctive style of life, exhibiting a generalized "gentlemanly" or "ladylike" posture of nonprofessionalism, and abiding by restrictions on social intercourse with non-upper-class members.

Strategic elites, however, are defined by their occupations and nothing else. They do not partake of separate cultural lifestyles distinct from those imposed by their occupations, or from that of the larger society. In Keller's words, "the President of the United States, the president of a giant corporation, the top atomic scientist, and the leading writer of an era have little in common beyond their general cultural background and their achievement of prominence" (1991, p. 83).

Lacking a common upper-class milieu, American elites also lack a common system of values for ruling, beyond that of the general culture. Acquiring the relevant value orientation among American elites occurs through both a process of anticipatory socialization and the lengthy process of occupational entry and promotion. The longer one stays in an occupation, all other things being equal, the more one accepts the value orientation of that profession. As a result, Keller finds that societies such as ours, with multiple strategic elites, have less social cohesion and value consensus compared with societies dominated by an upper class (1991, p. 141). Sociologist Allen Barton (1975) also found in his sample of elites that current occupations was the most significant predictor of current beliefs.

Strategic elites thus have less value cohesion than an upper class. In the case of contemporary American elites, this leads us into a discussion of ideology, American elites, and the (predominantly) conservative critique of the cultural sector. The argument of conservative intellectuals is that some American elites no longer support the traditional status quo. Prior to the New Deal, as Baltzell points out, the upper class was deeply conservative in attachment to traditional American institutions and to the rugged individualism of laissez-faire capitalism. During the Great Depression, members of this "caste" exhibited great personal hostility to President Franklin Delano Roosevelt as well as to his New Deal reforms, which created countervailing institutions of governmental power (Baltzell, 1966, pp. 226–59). The New Deal's success led to the widespread acceptance of a more liberal worldview, even among American elites after World War II. The general consensus at the top, however, remained stable until the 1960s. The rise and institutionalization of the adversary culture put an end to this consensus.

The adversary culture results from the value diversity inherent in a system of strategic elites—as opposed to an upper class—but at the same time, the adversary culture intensifies the value conflicts among elites. Chapter three discusses the nature of the ideological cleavages among elites.

THREE

THE STRUCTURE OF IDEOLOGY

This chapter focuses on how much the *values* of various American elite groups differ from each other. While pluralists argue that American elites are multiple and competing, they have little to say about elite values. Keller's discussion of elites and society (1991) suggests that elites differ greatly in terms of their attitudes and values, because of the structure of modern society and the principles of specialization and division of labor.

According to Keller (1991), as the division of labor and its concomitant occupational specialization expands, elite consensus necessarily declines as each group tends to focus on its particular tasks to the exclusion of all else, leading to a fragmented structure.[1] While we expect our elites to support general American values, Keller suggests that each elite group holds its own distinctive view of American life:

> Since strategic elites have different functions, facilities, and personnel, they emphasize and influence different aspects of the moral system. The members of each elite share and emphasize a distinctive set of values which represents a special sector of the collective life. . . . These elites are . . . subject to *general* legal and moral norms—they are expected to be law-abiding citizens, virtuous, and honorable. But each elite has its own special definitions and criteria of these virtues. (p. 141)

Yet, she argues, if society is to work at all, it must have a common moral order—without that, society is anomic and individuals have no meaning to their lives. Keller then contends that modern strategic elites have the capacity to hold together the larger cultural system (she uses the term *moral order*): "What is required for effective social life is moral accord among the strategic elites; they must have some loyalties and goals in common. As societies become more differentiated, a considerable degree of cohesion and consensus is needed at the top" (p. 146).

Most literature on elites, however, is not concerned with a lack of moral cohesion among strategic elites. Writers about elites tend to view them as supporting the fundamental values in American society. Disagreements are essentially over issues of policy. Dye characterizes the common elite framework as one of "liberal and public-regarding":

> By this we mean that institutional leaders have shown a willingness to take the welfare of others into account as an aspect of their own sense of well-being: they have been willing to use governmental power to correct perceived wrongs done to others. . . . The liberal establishment believes that it can change people's lives through the exercise of governmental power: end discrimination, abolish poverty, eliminate slums, ensure employment, uplift the poor, eliminate sickness, educate the masses, and instill dominant culture values in all citizens. (1986, p. 221)

Other critics have analyzed what they see as the contemporary American crisis by relating it to divisions among various elite groups. According to Daniel Bell (1978, pp. 46–52), the great moral divide began with the cultural movement of "modernism" over one hundred years ago and became dominant in the last half of the twentieth century. This view sees the fundamental conflict in American society as one between the traditional bourgeois culture and what Lionel Trilling first called the "adversary culture":[2]

> Any historian of the literature of the modern age will take virtually for granted the adversary intention, the actually subversive intention, that characterizes modern writing—he will perceive its clear purpose of detaching the reader from the habits of thought and feeling that the larger culture imposes, of giving him a ground and a vantage point from which to judge and condemn, and perhaps revise, the culture that has produced him. (pp. xii–xiii)

On the one hand, Bell extends the scope of the adversary culture well beyond literature to include all cultural occupations broadly defined. On the other hand, the bourgeoisie, the American majority, "has no intellectually respectable culture of its own—no major figures in literature, painting, or poetry—to counterpose to the adversary culture" (p. 41). The adversary elite dominates all aspects of American culture—publishers, the media, opinion makers, education, theater, music, television, and academia.

Social critic Irving Kristol also claims that America is dominated by new liberal ("adversarial") elites. According to Kristol, these new elites fundamentally despise capitalism, a social fact that corporate businesspeople have difficulty grasping:

> On any single day, all over the country, there are gatherings of corporate executives in which bewilderment and vexation are expressed at the climate of hostility toward business to be found in Washington, or in the media, or in academia—or even, incredibly, among their own children. (1978, p. 23)

These new elites, Kristol argues, think the national government must play a large role in satisfying the needs of the citizen. The free market is not enough. Moreover, these elites do not wish to change the society by persuading its citizens to refine and uplift their tastes and habits which, "supposedly, is the democratic way" (p. 27). Instead, they would rather

> mobilize the active layers of public opinion behind such issues as environmentalism, ecology, consumer protection, and economic planning, to give the governmental bureaucracy the power to regulate and coerce, and eventually to "politicize" the economic decision-making process. And this is, of course, exactly what has been happening. (p. 27)

Echoing a similar theme, political scientist Aaron Wildavsky attributes current conflict to the rise of an egalitarian culture, which he sees as adversarial. "Recent cultural conflict," he claims, "takes place through the decline of established orders and the rise of a critical culture—critical because egalitarian" (1991, p. 102). It attacks the values of hierarchy and individualism, which Wildavsky believes form the basis of contemporary American bourgeois society. Egalitarian culture attacks the notion of individual differences, individual talents, and individual achievements. It prescribes as the only legitimate social order an equality of result and proposes that authority (i.e., government) be directed solely toward achieving this end (1991, p. 103), while at the same time egalitarianism contributes to public distrust of government.

> Egalitarians make contradictory demands that demoralize government. On the one hand, they want government to do a great deal more. . . . On the other hand, since they believe leadership is suspect because it signifies an unequal relationship with followers, they constantly seek to undermine authority. The egalitarian desire for bu-

reaucracy without authority is not good for democratic government. (1991, p. xxxi)

To some critics the groups who have created the adversarial culture (however defined) constitute a "new class."

THE "NEW CLASS"

Marxists see class as the source of conflict and cleavage in all systems. They tend to equate class position, social status, and societal power. But as sociologist Max Weber (among others) points out, wealth, power, and status are not of a piece.

Weber (1946a) defines class in terms of economic position in the marketplace: producer versus consumer, creditor versus debtor, and owner (or manager) versus worker. Economic relations, while important, are not necessarily determinants of status group membership. That is, members of a class need not view themselves as such, nor does membership in a class necessarily lead to organized political action on that basis (1946a).

Weber defines a status group as a group of individuals who possess a common lifestyle, a shared consciousness of belonging to a distinct group, with a similar degree of social honor. The status order, unlike the marketplace, is stratified according to social honor rather than money, wealth, or property (although status groups are not unaffected by these economic interests).

Moreover, status groups differ in their degree of monopolization. In the extreme case, they become castes, which are often based on ethnic or racial differences. Occupational groups can also be status groups if they differ in their approved lifestyles, develop a distinctive consciousness of kind, and share a similar sense of social honor (Weber, 1946a, pp. 180–95). In Weber's sense of the term *status group*, the adversary culture is part of the lifestyle of a status group, namely intellectuals and those with intellectual pretensions.

From a different perspective, James Burnham modifies an economic class analysis by focusing on managerial and technical elites as new ruling groups in modern society. He argues in *The Managerial Revolution* (1942) that the capitalist system would decline and be replaced by a society controlled economically and politically by a managerial class. Burnham's analysis rests on the assumption that there exists a small, unified ruling class. Nevertheless, he argues that the basis of power of this new class is based not on the ownership of the corporation but on its management. In other words, power rests on control over, not ownership of, the means of production. The crisis of advanced capitalism, according to Burnham, is a product of the division between the owners of productive forces and those who direct the actual means of production. The owners have retired to spend the profits from their corporations without contributing to production, as the corporation itself has come under control of the managerial class, a technical elite with counterparts in the government bureaucracy. This new managerial elite depends no longer on the financial structure of modern capitalism but rather on the technical nature of modern production. The Marxist dichotomy between state and economy becomes meaningless, as the new managerial elite in the public and private sectors becomes interchangeable in the public and private sectors becomes interchangeable in knowledge, skill, and specialization.

From a very different point of view, several radical critics of the social order hope for the growth of such a noneconomic-based vanguard to transform America. In 1960, C. Wright Mills wrote:

> It is with the problem of agency [the mainspring of social change] in mind that I have been studying, for several years, the cultural apparatus, the intellectuals—as a possible, immediate radical agency of change . . . it turns out now, in the spring of 1960, that it may be a very relevant idea indeed. (as quoted in Bell, 1980, p. 140)

Recent "new class" theorists similarly argue that the ideological divisions between these new groups and traditional American elites reflect a larger conflict of class-based interests. The interests of the new class involve maintaining or increasing the privileges of knowledge-based authority. These interests naturally are in conflict with the interests of the business elites who seek to maximize profits. Symptomatic of the conflict is the tension between creators of modern film who see film as art and business elites who see film as a business. Both conservatives and liberal "new class" theorists define the new class in terms of its opposition to competitive, profit-seeking, materialistic culture of the more traditional classes.

Marxist sociologist Alvin Gouldner, for example, wrote of a new class composed of intelligentsia and technical intelligentsia (1979). This new class is in conflict with the groups that already control the economy (business executives). The source of conflict, Gouldner argues, is ultimately rooted in the respective positions of these classes in the social structure.

Political scientist Ronald Inglehart (1977) identifies the emerging new class of postindustrial society with "postmaterialist" (or "postbourgeois") values, such as "self-actualization," freer personal life, environmental concerns, the democratization of work and personal life, and greater participation in idealistic politics. Traditional classes, however, are more concerned with material satisfactions—economic growth, safety and reducing crime, a stable economy, and a higher standard of living.

Political scientist Scott Flanagan (1979) has identified similar kinds of postbourgeois versus bourgeois values in advanced industrial democracies. He argues that the transition to postindustrial society has created a new stratum and a new set of postindustrial values as a function of advanced technology. The change has been along four dimensions: from frugality to self-indulgence, pietism to secularism, conformity to independence, and devotion to authority to self-assertiveness.

Why do the members of the new class hold antibourgeois values? Despite widely varying ideologies, most writers on the new class see the conflict as a long-term struggle for power between the old class and the new (for writings on the new class, see Schumpeter, 1950; Kristol, 1978; Gouldner, 1979; Ehrenreich and Ehrenreich, 1977; Wuthnow and Shrum, 1977; Berger, 1985; and McAdams, 1987; see also the articles in Bruce-Briggs 1979).

Most writings on the new class argue that it desires to increase its power at the expense of business. This is the agenda behind its liberal attitudes. The liberalism of the new class, with its desire to expand the reach of government as a countervailing power to that of business, is the ideological club by which the new class attacks its enemy, the American business elite and the capitalist system of which it is the emblem, and thus furthers its own interests and power.

Critics of the concept of new class contend, however, that the underlying assumptions of the new class argument confuse the causal relationship between class and ideology (Bell, 1980; Bazelon, 1967; Brint, 1984). "New class" analysis blends together two social facts. One is the fact of new occupations and professions based on bureaucracy, technical specialization, and knowledge. The second social fact is the widespread diffusion of a worldview, values, and attitudes critical of the bourgeois capitalist order.

It is true that the white-collar occupations (professional, managerial, technical, sales, and clerical jobs) have expanded in size and influence. Fewer than one in five working Americans held white-collar jobs at the turn of the century, compared with more than half in the 1990s.

Correspondingly, white-collar professionals have also been more liberal in voting behavior and general political attitudes. In the 1970s, white-collar managers and professionals were the most liberal of occupational groups on most economic, social, and foreign policy issues (Ladd, 1978; Lipset, 1981, pp. 502–23). Despite the general shift to the right during the 1980s (this stratum included), college graduates with white-collar jobs remain the most liberal stratum.[3]

But correlation need not be causation. Sociologist Michael Macy concludes that "instead of shaping the ideology of incumbents, social cultural occupations"—the locus of Kristol's new class—"appear to serve as a cache area for the adversary culture, providing an attractive alternative" to employment elsewhere (1988, p. 348).

Similarly, Bell argues that the rise of liberalism among these white-collar professions is not a necessary concomitant of a rising class conflict between the bourgeois and a new class. For a variety of reasons, the liberalism of the white-collar occupations is the most extreme and visible case of a societywide trend.

> The "new class" consists of individuals who have carried the logic of modern culture to its end. Serious and committed, as many are, or trendy and chic as others may be, they make up a cultural phenomenon that mirrors the breakdown of traditional values in Western society. It is not a "new class" in any social-structural sense. It is the endpoint of a culture in disarray. (Bell, 1980, p. 162)

While a test of various "new class" theses is beyond the scope of this book, the general notion of the rise of a new class does suggest that occupations anchored in the production and transmission of ideas and symbols are more critical of the American system than are traditional leadership groups. If this is true we should find sharp cleavages among elite groups in American society, and the fault line of these cleavages should lie between traditional elites and the new or newly powerful cultural elites.

THE CONCEPT OF IDEOLOGY

How does one define ideology? The answer to this question is important because the concept has been defined in many different ways. One group of social critics defines ideology as a systematic collection of distorted thought, a set of proposals, theories, and aims that form a political program with implications of propagandizing (i.e., Communism, Nazism). When we accuse someone of having an ideology, we implicitly accuse him or her of being rigid, dogmatic, utopian, nonpragmatic, and ultimately totalitarian in personality and behavior: a true believer. As the saying goes, "I have a social philosophy, you have political opinions, he has an ideology."[4] Ideology in this sense has definite utopian, deceptive, and coercive connotations.[5]

Because many Americans associate ideology with utopian thinking, they tend not to think of mainstream American politics as being ideological. While the two main political parties may have their policy differences, the argument goes, the parties manage to settle these differences through the art of compromise and negotiation. It is this type of compromise orientation that sets American politics apart from the more "ideological" politics of the rest of the world.

Ideology has also been taken to mean a set of values and ideas that rationalize self-interest, which is, therefore, somehow antithetical to the common good. In this view of ideology, people act in pursuit of interest, and the sociopolitical universe is a struggle between interests. Ironically, many pluralist theorists such as Dahl share this assumption with Marxists. In both views groups ultimately act in pursuit of their own interests. Ideology, as a set of values, ideas, and attitudes, is the mechanism that both reflects and disguises this pursuit. Some liberal pluralists and Marxists differ primarily in how ideologies are produced by what kind of groups. Marxists associate ideologies with social classes only, while pluralists argue that there is a wide range of social groups that create ideologies.

For the more psychologically oriented, ideology, particularly conservative ideology, is a manifestation of a defective personality type. Members of the Frankfurt school, for example, argue that ideology is associated with personality type. Research in the area of family and personality psychology came together in an overall developmental theory of the potentially fascist personality. The intent of the Frankfurt school, manifest in the famous study of the authoritarian personality, was to alert Americans to the potential fascist threat in their midst (see, for example, Rothman and Lichter, 1982).

Some scholars argue that the so-called personality trait of authoritarianism is really a set of working-class antidemocratic attitudes, which are class and cultural in origin and have little to do with underlying psychological characteristics. This is the position advanced by Lipset (1981). Surveys using an instrument called the F scale repeatedly show that lower-status people are less committed to democratic ideals, more attracted to extremist movements, and more imbued with political and social conservatism than are upper-status persons (Lipset, 1981).

Other scholars criticize such studies of ideology and personality for treating conservatism and authoritarian attitudes as parallel concepts. Is authoritarianism merely a reflection of an extremely conservative ideology? Sociologist Edward Shils criticizes the F scale as measuring "political attitudes masquerading as personality dispositions . . . designed to disclose not authoritarian personality as such but rather the 'Right'—the nativist-fundamentalist-authoritarian" (1956, p. 158).[6]

In this book, we use yet another definition of ideology. Anthropolgist Clifford Geertz, in his classic essay "Ideology as a Cultural System" (1973, pp. 193–233), defines ideology in a nonevaluative, nonpsychological, and nonhistoricist manner. He makes ideology a public, shared phenomenon rather than a subjective set of ideas embedded within the mind of the individual. Ideologies, according to Geertz, are systems of meaning that attempt both to make sense of the social and political world and to provide a set of prescriptions for thought and action. They are cultural phenomena, and are not to be taken as merely derivative of either personality or social structure. Ideologies are social metaphors that operate like scientific paradigms, explaining a multitude of ideas with a few phrases and sentences.

Sociologist Ann Swidler (1986) distinguishes between two polar types of cultural systems. Where custom, ritual, and tradition dominate, social life is unexamined; this culture is uncontested and consensual (p. 278). Consensual cultural systems do not require intellectuals or philosophers. Swidler also describes a second type of culture, contested culture, which aligns with Geertz's notion of ideology as a cultural system. In periods of massive social change, the "established" culture is rejected, only to be replaced by alternative, and sometimes conflicting, views of action (ibid.). Ideology comes into play when the traditional bases of understanding and action lose their force. It is ideology's articulate, unifying nature that makes it an attractive guide for action when the old culture no longer works. This is also why ideologies need intellectuals to provide the explicit arguments.

Even the most radical new ideologies, however, always draw on previous cultural patterns. Rarely, if ever, is the past completely rejected. Indeed, ideologies cannot help but draw from previous cultural assumptions, Swidler notes: "Ideological movements are not complete cultures, in the sense that much of their taken-for-granted understanding of the world and many of their daily practices still depend on traditional patterns" (p. 279).

Broad-gauged ideologies emerge when the society and culture no longer mesh. Swidler makes the point that social science lacks explanations for why some groups of people adopt one ideology, while others choose another:

Explaining cultural outcomes . . . requires not only understanding the direct influence of an ideology on action. It also requires explaining why one ideology rather than another triumphs (or at least endures). And such explanation depends on analyzing the structural constraints and historical circumstances within which ideological movements struggle for dominance. (p. 280)[7]

MODERN AMERICAN LIBERALISM VERSUS MODERN AMERICAN CONSERVATISM

The terms *liberal* and *conservative* are commonly used in several different ways that must be distinguished. For example, the term *liberal* describes an Anglo-American political tradition. Scholars of political philosophy and history call the tradition of political thought beginning with John Locke, Montesquieu, and Jefferson and extending to the present "the liberal tradition," or classical liberalism. Textbooks such as Sabine (1961) and such academic treatments as otherwise different as Watkins (1948), Minogue (1963), and Holmes (1993) use the term *liberalism* in this fashion. Political theorist Stephen Holmes characterizes Anglo-American liberal practice as consisting of religious tolerance, free speech, limits on police power, free elections, the separation of powers, private property, and freedom of contract (1933, p. 4).

While this is a common designation in academic political theory, it is not the sense in which most of us usually use the term *liberal*. In fact, confusion between these two usages is rife. Contemporary American liberals and contemporary American conservatives alike derive a good part of their substance and argument from the broader liberal tradition. Neither desire a formal state church nor national theocracy. Both sides share a belief in political democracy and free elections. Both sides believe in the rule of law, the separation of powers, and due process, although American liberals and conservatives sharply disagree on many other issues.

Moreover, Americans do not use the term *liberalism* in the same way that Europeans do. In fact, classical European liberalism more closely resembles what we (and what Americans generally) call conservatism. The left in America is not the same as the left in Europe, and the right in America is also not the same as the right in Europe. The American left and right both partake of the classical Lockean liberal tradition; the European left and right do not. The European division of left and right dates from the time of the French Revolution (and the seating arrangements at the French National Assembly). The left is the inheritor of the

Jacobin tradition, while the right derives from the defense of the ancien régime. Contemporary American liberalism is left of center, and that which distinguishes Mario Cuomo's politics from the conservatism of Ronald Reagan.

Additional confusion characterizes discussions of American conservatism, insofar as a person can be either a programmatic conservative or a nonideological, temperamental conservative. Conservatives by temperament are those to whom John Stuart Mill refers when he calls conservatives stupid. In his treatise *Consideration on Representative Government,* Mill states: "Conservatives, as being by the law of their existence the stupidest party, have much the greater sins of this description to answer for" (1972 ed., p. 261). Sociologist Karl Mannheim (1971) makes a similar assertion: conservatism, according to him, is not an ideology at all but is bound up with traditional modes of action, that is, the taken-for-granted world.

Irving Kristol, prominent neoconservative intellectual, also equates that kind of conservatism with a mere liking for things traditional. Like all traditional modes, Kristol argues, American conservatism is instinctive and unreflective; it sensitizes persons to particulars, not to abstract ideas. This affinity to the particulars makes conservatives resistant to the lures of ideological thinking.

This type of conservative is clearly suspicious of change. He or she believes in such clichés as "If it ain't broke, don't fix it," and "If it is not necessary to change, it is necessary not to change." As a result, Kristol speculates, this affinity renders the conservative averse to abstract, far-reaching innovations (1978, p. 121). Ironically, this aversion to speculative thought is, in his view, responsible for American conservatism's relative lack of intellectual depth and thus its relative lack of success in the past.[8]

In repeated studies of the general public, political scientists find that only a few Americans think clearly and without prompting about political issues, political parties, and candidates in ideological terms, conservative or liberal. Philip Converse, in his classic study of American voter ideology (1964), found that only one in forty voters use any kind of abstract concept (e.g., "affirmative action, free enterprise, law and order, extremist, isolationism") to evaluate candidates. Others (Nie, Verba, and Petrocik, 1976; Neuman, 1986) have found proportionately more ideologues—up to 17 percent of the general public by the mid-seventies. The overwhelming majority of the voting public, however, choose candidates based on narrow (and undefined) group interest (e.g., is he good for labor?), or on what Converse calls "the nature of the times (e.g., has the

economy gotten better or worse?)," or lastly, on purely personal characteristics (for more discussion, see Lerner, Nagai, and Rothman, 1991;
Sniderman, 1993).

Nonideological thinking of this type is a form of traditionalism that
should not be confused with programmatic conservatism. Because traditionalism is instinctive and unreflective, it will naturally lead individuals
to support the status quo, whatever that status quo may be. While the
two kinds of conservatism are probably empirically related, we use the
term *conservative* in this book to refer to a programmatic set of positions
and not a temperament.

The confusion of terms is rooted in recent American history, for the
modern standardization of political terminology only began with the
New Deal era. According to Rotunda (1986), Herbert Hoover and Franklin Roosevelt both defined themselves as liberals. Robert Taft and Harry
Truman followed suit. Nonetheless, modern America was set in place by
the New Deal. American conservatism as an intellectually inspired, ideological movement began after World War II (see also Nash, 1976).

All of this is by way of introduction. The confusions and uncertain-
ties of terminologies require explicit empirical analysis in order to understand what liberal and conservative actually mean when used to describe
existing political positions. Our approach here is to explore the ideological divisions among American elites as revealed in the surveys discussed
earlier. We will demonstrate that these divisions are powerful predictors
of other attitudes and self-reported voting behavior.

THE CONTENT OF AMERICAN ELITE IDEOLOGY

While our everyday language uses the words *conservative* and *liberal* or
right and *left* to imply the existence of a single ideological dimension,
political scientists and sociologists have long known that political ideology is a multidimensional construct. At least as early as Seymour Lipset's
classic book *Political Man*, social scientists distinguished between "economic" and noneconomic or "social" liberalism (1981, orig. 1959; see
also Berelson, Lazarsfeld, and McPhee, 1954, pp. 182–214). By the latter
term Lipset meant "civil liberties, race, and foreign affairs" (p. 318). In
1970, Richard Scammon and Ben Wattenberg's *The Real Majority* made
the case that since the majority of Americans were "unyoung, unpoor,
and unblack," the key for a Democrat in winning the White House was to
avoid discussing these social issues and focus on economic issues. Other
scholars have tended either to keep this dichotomy (e.g., Lipset, 1981;
Barton and Parsons, 1977; Verba and Orren, 1985; McClosky and Zaller,

1984) or to expand it to include foreign policy, civil rights, and cultural issues (e.g., Lieske, 1991, pp. 181–82).

However, most of these discussions have treated noneconomic issues as ad hoc additions to the conflict over the proper extent of the welfare state, possibly because of a lingering attachment to the notion that in the last analysis all issues are fundamentally economic. While not wishing to discount the importance of economic issues, we believe that other pressing issues like gay rights, abortion, crime, prayer in school, and American military intervention abroad are important enough to be treated systematically in their own right. Our strategy for isolating these distinct dimensions of liberalism does not impose any kind of a priori order on issue positions. The dimensions we describe are obtained from our findings on the interrelation of the elites' beliefs.

The strategy has a second advantage as well. Thinking of ideology as consisting of several independent dimensions allows us to accommodate the possibility that an individual can hold liberal opinions on some issues and conservative opinions on others in a systematic manner. For example, Gov. William Weld of Massachusetts is a liberal on issues of expressive individualism and a conservative on issues of collectivist liberalism: that is, he is a libertarian. Oddly, some scholars maintain that multidimensional analyses are unsatisfactory because they conceal the underlying unity of an ideological position (e.g., Wildavsky, 1991). In contrast, we believe that such analyses increase our understanding, because they capture the complexity of belief systems.[9]

THE FACTOR ANALYSES

The statistical technique of factor analysis allows us to begin with the question responses and to extract the underlying dimensions that constitute core beliefs. These represent certain underlying values that link otherwise seemingly disparate attitude questions into what we generally call modern conservatism versus modern liberalism. The dimensions are ideal-type abstractions meant to represent and partially explicate the underlying link between otherwise disparate issue positions.

The technique enables us to group these responses into four underlying dimensions of ideology: laissez-faire individualism versus collectivist liberalism; traditional Puritanism versus expressive individualism; system loyalty versus system alienation; and regime threat versus no regime threat.

We asked our respondents about various political, social, and economic issues. All twelve elite groups were asked a common set of seventeen attitudinal questions. In 1979 the first elite groups surveyed—the media and corporate business elites—answered the seventeen questions used in this analysis, as well as others not analyzed here. Subsequently, the movie and television elites also responded to these seventeen questions, and eight different ones not used here. The remaining eight groups were asked the seventeen standard questions, plus thirteen others. (See the appendix for complete question wordings. All responses took the form of a four-point Likert scale, "strongly agree," "somewhat agree," "somewhat disagree," and "strongly disagree.")

Our procedure is more complicated than is desirable because of question rotation. Since all twelve elite groups were asked a common set of seventeen questions, we performed an initial factor analysis on all the groups with these common questions. This yielded three distinct factors: collectivist liberalism, system alienation, and expressive individualism. We present first the three dimensions that emerged from our twelve-group, seventeen-question factor analysis.

We later performed a second factor analysis on the eight elite groups that were asked the seventeen questions plus the additional thirteen. We will discuss the additional factor that emerged using all thirty questions on the eight elite groups.

We followed the same procedure for both analyses. We performed a particular kind of factor analysis, common factors, allowing the extraction of all factors whose eigenvalues were greater than one. We then subjected the retained factors to a varimax rotation and examined the factor loadings to discern the pattern of loadings. Questions were retained on a factor if they had a loading of 0.44 or more (see Table 3.1 for a list of questions and their loadings), except for one case in which a question with a slightly lower loading was clearly part of the factor on which it loaded, and loaded on no other factor. To test the stability of the resulting dimensions, we performed a separate analysis on each dimension. To construct scales for subsequent analysis, we used the regression method to obtain the factor score coefficients—which play a role analogous to multiple regression coefficients in ordinary regression analysis—to compute factor scores for new variables which were saved and used in subsequent analyses.

Statistically minded readers may wonder why we used principal factors as our technique of analysis, when the trend is to use principle components analysis. We chose this approach because we believe that the core values of ideology are underlying latent variables, not to be mistaken for the indicators that are measured with error. This is especially important for ideology since many of the specific objects that

TABLE 3.1   Attitudinal Items for Four Ideological Dimensions

Collectivist Liberalism	Loading
The government should work to substantially reduce the income gap between the rich and the poor	−0.58
It is not the proper role of government to insure that everyone has a job	0.48
Less government regulation of business would be good for the country	0.46
Our environmental problems are not as serious as people have been led to believe	0.36

Expressive Individualism	Loading
It is a woman's right to decide whether or not to have an abortion	−0.51
Homosexuals should not be allowed to teach in public schools	0.58
It is wrong for a married person to have sexual relations with someone other than his or her spouse	0.52
It is wrong for adults of the same sex to have sexual relations	0.79

System Alienation	Loading
The American legal system mainly favors the wealthy	0.47
The American private enterprise system is generally fair to working people	−0.44
The United states needs a complete restructuring of its basic institutions	0.60
Big corporations should be taken out of private ownership and run in the public intersest	0.44
The structure of our society causes most people to feel alienated	0.56
The main goal of U.S. foreign policy has been to protect U.S. business interests	0.50

Regime Threat	Loading
It is sometimes necessary for the CIA to protect U.S. interests by undermining hostile governments	0.48
We should be more forceful in our dealings with the Soviet Union even if it increases the risk of war	0.59
It is important for America to have the strongest military force in the world, no matter what it costs	0.58
There is too much concern in the courts for the rights of criminals	0.56

Note: Factor loadings for the first three factors are taken from the twelve elite group factor analysis, while those of the fourth are taken from the eight elite group factor analysis.

engage ideological interest change, disappear (e.g., the Soviet Union), or cease to be public policy issues. New concerns also emerge, adding to the complex mix of actively considered issues. Our argument is that ideological predispositions are more enduring than the specific objects of individual concern. Common factor analysis is methodologically appropriate for this situation, unlike principal components. We did, however, replicate the factor analyses using the principal components technique and found a nearly identical patterning of factor loadings (not shown here).[10]

The Three Initial Dimensions of Ideology

Table 3.1 shows our factor analysis on all twelve elite groups with the set of seventeen questions. We label the three ideological dimensions as follows: laissez-faire individualism versus collectivist liberalism; traditional Puritanism versus expressive individualism; and system loyalty versus system alienation. For the sake of convenience, we often refer to an individual dimension by the label we have assigned to its liberal pole (e.g., collectivist liberalism, expressive individualism, system alienation).

LAISSEZ-FAIRE INDIVIDUALISM VERSUS COLLECTIVIST LIBERALISM.   Four items tap into this dimension, often dealing with economics and welfare-state issues. We discuss the dimension itself and its social correlates in greater detail later in the book, but list the significant items here:

- The government should work to substantially reduce the income gap between the rich and the poor.
- It is not the proper role of government to insure that everyone has a job.
- Less government regulation of business would be good for the country.
- Our environmental problems are not as serious as people have been led to believe.

Disagreement with the first item and agreement with the other three constitute the conservative response. The liberal position maintains that government should reduce the income gap, insure jobs, and increase regulation, but at the same time believes in the seriousness of environmental problems.

TRADITIONAL PURITANISM VERSUS EXPRESSIVE INDIVIDUALISM.   Four items are associated with another dimension of ideology, which we label traditional Puritanism versus expressive individualism. The issues that connected with this second dimension are:

- It is a woman's right to decide whether or not to have an abortion.
- Lesbians and homosexuals should not be allowed to teach in public schools.
- It is wrong for a married person to have sexual relations with someone other than his or her spouse.
- It is wrong for adults of the same sex to have sexual relations.[11]

Disagreement with the first item and agreement with the rest mark traditional values, while the opposite set of responses relates to the core value of expressive individualism.

SYSTEM LOYALTY VERSUS SYSTEM ALIENATION.   Six questions constitute this third dimension:

- The American legal system mainly favors the wealthy.
- The American private enterprise system is generally fair to working
  · people.
- The United States needs a complete restructuring of its basic institutions.
- Big corporations should be taken out of private ownership and run in the public interest.
- The structure of our society causes most people to feel alienated.
- The main goal of American foreign policy has been to protect U.S. business interests.

Agreement with the second question and disagreement with the remaining questions constitute system loyalty, while the opposite set of responses comprises the system alienation position.[12]

A Fourth Ideological Dimension

The second factor analysis was done on eight groups, using a set of thirty questions. This richer set of questions yielded an additional ideological dimension, which we label regime threat. In addition, two questions on affirmative action were highly correlated with each other and nothing else; that is, they did not load on any of the ideological dimensions or even correlate with other questions related to racial issues. The matter is of importance only because it replicates for elites the findings for the general population by Sniderman and Piazza (1993). Opposition to affirmative action seems to indicate American notions of fairness that transcend the liberal conservative ideological dimension and differences in racial attitudes.[13]

The second factor analysis also replicated the earlier three dimensions. Expressive individualism emerged with the same questions loading on the factor. The statement "Women with young children shouldn't work outside the home unless it is financially necessary" loaded as well. Agreement constitutes the moral traditionalism response, while disagreement indicates expressive individualism.

REGIME THREAT. The regime threat dimension is intriguing and novel. We call this dimension regime threat because we think it taps into the degree to which a person feels threatened by the outside world, whether it be on the international sphere (resulting in a strong anti-Communist response) or by the violation of system norms (causing a strong reaction against perceived leniency toward criminals). The following four questions loaded on this dimension.

- It is sometimes necessary for the CIA to protect U.S. interests by undermining hostile governments.
- We should be more forceful in our dealings with the Soviet Union even if it increases the risk of war.
- It is important for America to have the strongest military force in the world, no matter what it costs.
- There is too much concern in the courts for the rights of criminals.

Agreement with these questions constitutes the conservative or regime threat response, while disagreement with them constitutes the liberal or no regime threat response. If we followed our usual practice of naming the dimension for its liberal side, we would call the overall dimension the "no regime threat" dimension; however, in the interests of clarity, we instead refer to it as the "regime threat" dimension. We discuss this dimension in greater detail in chapter seven, which considers the adversary culture.[14]

IDEOLOGICAL DIVISIONS AMONG AMERICAN ELITES

Our survey of the American elite shows that its members are ideologically polarized. First, we examine how those at the top label themselves ideologically. We then compare them on the four ideological dimensions captured by the factor analysis.

Self-Identified Ideology

Conservative, moderate, and *liberal* are standard terms Americans use to categorize political opinions. We asked all of our respondents the standard public opinion question, to describe their political views on a seven-point scale, from one ("conservative") to seven ("liberal"), with four labeled as "middle-of-the-road."

On the basis of their self-definitions, the American elite are somewhat split along a conservative-liberal continuum. Eighteen percent la-

TABLE 3.2   Self-Identified Ideology Among American Elites (percentage)

	Conservative	Moderate	Liberal	N
Bureaucrats	27	17	56	199
Business	63	23	14	242
Congressional aides	37	11	52	133
Judges	23	22	54	112
Labor	6	20	73	94
Lawyers	32	22	47	148
Media	17	28	55	232
Military	77	14	9	152
Movies	19	14	67	90
Public interest	1	8	91	151
Religious leaders	26	15	59	174
Television	14	12	75	103
Average	31	18	51	1,830

bel themselves middle-of-the-road, while 51 percent call themselves liberal and 31 percent think of themselves as conservatives. Ideological differences are greater when elites are divided by occupation (see Table 3.2). Ninety-one percent of the public interest elite, roughly three out of four makers of prime-time television and labor leaders, and majorities of religious leaders, filmmakers, bureaucrats, the media elite, federal judges, and congressional aides call themselves liberal. At the other end of the ideological scale, only 9 percent of the military leaders and 14 percent of the business executives refer to themselves as liberal.[15]

The Factor Dimensions

For most members of the American elite, ideological labels of conservative, moderate, and liberal translate into predictably conservative, moderate, and liberal responses to specific questions. Significant differences among elite groups emerge especially when we compare traditional versus new occupational elites. To facilitate discussion, we created a score for each respondent, on each ideological dimension as described earlier. The scores are normalized so that the mean of each scale is set at 100 and its standard deviation at 10. Scores greater than 100 indicate greater liberalism while scores less than 100 indicate greater conservatism.

The collectivist liberalism dimension contrasts rugged individualism with collectivist welfare-state liberalism. In the total sample, individual scores range from an extremely conservative score of 70.65 to an extremely liberal 126.21. Table 3.3 shows the large, statistically significant differences between elite groups. Scores range from a mean score of 109.91 for public interest group leaders to 92.22 for business executives, a difference of nearly two standard deviations. Not surprisingly, labor leaders are almost as liberal as the public interest elite. Business and military leaders are far more conservative than other groups, but they are followed closely by bureaucrats.[16]

The second dimension situates system loyalty against system alienation, with individual scores ranging from 78.16 to 128.81. The large differences between elite groups are also statistically significant. The least alienated groups (aside from lawyers) are in government and the business elite; this cluster of elites resembles C. Wright Mills's military-industrial complex. In contrast, the public interest leaders, labor, and cultural elites are alienated from the system. The differences between insider and outsider groups are almost all statistically significant. In fact, lawyers and public interest leaders are nearly 1.5 standard deviations apart.[17]

The expressive individualism dimension contrasts the traditional Puritanism of classical American liberals (today most often at least social and cultural conservatives) with the expressive individualism of contemporary liberals, especially those involved with the creation and distribution of culture. Scores range from 76.14 to 199.72. The elite occupational groups align closely with Daniel Bell's "pre- versus post-Modernism" cultural divide (1976). Religious leaders are the most conservative. Labor leaders, however, are more conservative than other liberal groups; the differences are statistically significant.

Public interest leaders and the elites of popular culture (television, news, and movies) are more liberal than everyone else, again with differences that are statistically significant. Social critics like William Bennett (1992) and Michael Medved (1992) accuse the cultural elites of being to the far left of most Americans. We find them to be on the left of most elites.[18]

The regime threat dimension contrasts conservatives' willingness to use force against those who are perceived as attacking the system, including moral norms, with liberals' apparent regard for such groups, either the Soviet Union or criminals, as not constituting a serious enough threat to justify the use of force. (A less benign interpretation, to be discussed later, might explain liberals' attitudes as a function of their own covert sympathy with such groups because of their own hostility to the system.) The scores on this factor range from 70.07 to 125.43. As expected, military leaders are the most conservative on the regime threat dimension, while

TABLE 3.3 Factor Scores with Scheffe Confidence Intervals for Four Ideological Dimensions

Collectivist Liberalism

Scores		Bus	Mil	Bur	Con	Law	TV	Mov	Med	Jud	Lab	Pub
92.22	Bus											
93.70	Mil											
94.41	Bur	*										
98.36	Con	*	*									
98.93	Law	*	*									
99.99	TV	*	*									
100.78	Mov	*	*									
101.43	Med	*	*									
102.06	Jud	*	*									
104.47	Rel	*	*	*	*	*						
105.07	Lab	*	*	*	*	*						
109.91	Pub	*	*	*	*	*	*	*	*	*		

Alienation

Scores		Law	Jud	Mil	Bur	Bus	Con	Med	Rel	TV	Lab	Mov	Pub
93.13	Law												
95.02	Jud												
95.40	Mil												
97.63	Bur	*											
97.75	Bus	*											
99.06	Con	*											
101.08	Med	*	*	*									
102.48	Rel	*	*	*	*	*							
104.18	TV	*	*	*	*	*							
105.28	Lab	*	*	*	*	*	*						
106.90	Mov	*	*	*	*	*	*	*					
107.79	Pub	*	*	*	*	*	*	*	*				

Expressive Individualism

Scores		Rel	Mil	Lab	Jud	Bus	Con	Law	Med	Mov	Pub	TV
91.12	Rel											
92.22	Mil											
96.27	Lab	*										
97.27	Jud	*	*									
98.90	Bus	*	*									
99.34	Con	*	*									
100.02	Bur	*	*									
103.39	Law	*	*	*	*	*						
105.52	Med	*	*	*	*	*	*	*				
105.90	Mov	*	*	*	*	*	*	*				
106.13	Pub	*	*	*	*	*	*	*				
106.32	TV	*	*	*	*	*	*	*				

continued

TABLE 3.3 *Continued*

		Regime Threat						
		Mil	Lab	Con	Bur	Law	Jud	Rel	Pub
90.86	Mil								
96.61	Lab	*							
97.97	Con	*							
99.14	Bur	*							
102.22	Law	*	*	*					
103.16	Jud	*	*	*	*				
103.30	Rel	*	*	*	*				
106.45	Pub	*	*	*	*	*			

$N = 1,715$

Note: Asterisk denotes pairs of groups significantly different at the 0.05 level of significance.
Abbreviations are as follows:

Bur	= Bureaucrats	Med	= News Media Elite
Bus	= Business Elites	Mil	= Military Elites
Con	= Congressional Aides	Mov	= Movie Elites
Jud	= Judges	Pub	= Leaders of Public Interest
Lab	= Labor Leaders		Organizations
Law	= Lawyers	TV	= Television Elites

public interest leaders have the most benign view of the "other." Labor leaders are the second most conservative of groups on this dimension, and significantly more so than the public interest elite and religious leaders.

Within the regime threat dimension, religious leaders (unlike all other groups) are extremely polarized between fundamentalist Protestant leaders and Catholics and mainline Protestants. Fundamentalists, with an average score of 95.97, are the most conservative group next to the military, while Roman Catholics at 104.78 and mainline Protestants at 105.25 are barely second in their liberalism to the most liberal elite group, public interest leaders.[19]

Given that liberalism is composed of these four dimensions, what do elites mean when they call themselves conservative, moderate, and lib-

TABLE 3.4   Ideological Dimensions as Predictors of Self-Reported Political View (standardized regression weights)

Alienation	0.31
Expressive individualism	0.24
Collective liberalism	0.35
Regime threat	0.20
R-squared	0.51

$N = 1,122$
Note: All values are significant at $p < 0.05$.

eral? The next section compares the correlations of self-identified liberalism with the four dimensions we derived. Self-identified liberalism correlates with each of these individual dimensions.[20]

In addition, the four dimensions of ideology identified by factor
analyses relate predictably to self-identified political view. Table 3.4
shows the results of a regression analysis of the relationship between the
ideological dimensions and self-identification. Taken together, the four
dimensions account for more than half of the variability in self-identified
political view. This suggests that the dimensions constitute much of the
foundation of self-identification. The meaning of the labels "liberal" and
"conservative" is built on the view of the world that is set out by the
ideological dimensions.

Table 3.4 shows that all of the dimensions are related to self-identified political view, as indicated by the magnitude of the standardized
weights (all are very different from zero). This indicates that all the
dimensions are needed to gain a full understanding of the underlying
structure of political view. None of the dimensions alone may be reduced
to the liberal-conservative continuum. This is evidence that ideology is,
indeed, more complex than can be captured in the familiar perspective.

In sum, the four dimensions of liberalism highlight some intriguing
conflicts among American elites. Focusing solely on economic issues
gives the wrong impression about conservatism versus liberalism in
America, for it puts labor leaders in the same liberal camp as public
interest leaders and secular cultural elites. The split is really between
adherents of what social critics call the adversary culture and elites who
believe in more traditional values. If we look at the issues of expressive
individualism (e.g., abortion, gay rights) or no regime threat versus
regime threat (e.g., crime), labor leaders are in the conservative camp.
Furthermore, unlike economic issues, these issues of expressive individualism and regime threat do not easily lend themselves to interest-based
legislative politics as usual.

FOUR

FOUR DIMENSIONS OF IDEOLOGY AND THEIR IMPACT

The idea that ideologies are systematic worldviews carries several impli-cations. Geertz and Swidler both argue that ideology should be consid-ered a distinct cultural system. If this is true, then the dimensions of American ideology, as defined by our factor analysis, should shape per-sons' views on political events and political personalities. We show how ideological positions predict elite views of various institutions, their rankings of America's most important societal goals, their view of media reliability, and their voting patterns.

THE RANKING OF INSTITUTIONS

We presented our elite group sample with a list of ten institutional groups, business leaders, the news media, intellectuals, labor unions, consumer groups, feminists, black leaders, federal government agencies, military leaders, and religious leaders. For each we asked our respon-dents to rate how much influence the group has and how much influence the group should have. The scales each range from one, very little influ-ence, to seven, a great deal of influence.

PERCEPTIONS OF GROUP INFLUENCE

If ideologies are general worldviews, then ideological positions should affect perceptions of what the world is, as well as visions of what the world ought to be. We do not expect ideological dispositions to affect perceptions of simple social facts, such as who won a particular presidential election. We do believe, however, that perceptions of social objects as complex as power relations are likely to be affected.

We expect that whatever their ideology, persons supportive of particular groups will believe that those they support have less power than other groups and should have more power relative to such groups. Specific hypotheses are easy to derive: liberals will tend to say that business, the military, and religion have much power and that labor, consumer groups, feminists, and black leaders have little power. Conservatives will take the opposite position. They will perceive that business, the military, and religion have little power, that adversarial institutions such as the media and intellectuals wield more power, and that challenging groups such as consumer groups, feminists, and black leaders have the most power.

To make such comparisons, we entered the factor scores for all the ideological dimensions into a regression equation for each institution with "degree of influence each institution has" as the dependent variable. Table 4.1 shows the standardized regression coefficients on each dimension for each institution. Comparison of the size of the standardized regression coefficients indicates which dimension underlies a person's assessment regarding how much power a particular group has.

The analysis of ideological dimensions and perceptions of power is complex. There is no simple formula for accounting how the ideological dimensions influence an individual's assessment of the power held by other groups. Our analysis shows, for example, that alienation and collectivist liberalism (the two factors with the largest standardized regression coefficients) have a greater impact on perceptions of business's power than the other ideological dimensions (see Table 4.1). Perceptions of the military's power are also strongly related to support for collectivist liberalism and degree of alienation from the system in the direction we suggested: the higher the liberalism and alienation scores, the greater the perceived influence of business or the military.

While system alienation is not related to assessment of labor's power, a high score on regime threat and, to a lesser extent, hostility toward collectivist liberalism are negatively related to perceived power scores for labor. To put it in somewhat different terms, if one supports a free-market economy or if one is concerned that outsider threats to one's community are important, then one thinks that labor has a great deal of power. Similarly, a lower score on the regime threat factor is associated with the view that consumer groups are relatively powerful.[1]

The regime threat dimension is also closely related to views on intellectuals (i.e., the variable has the largest standardized regression coeffi-

TABLE 4.1 Ideological Dimensions as Predictors of Perceived Power of Elite Groups (standardized regression weights)

						Criterion of Power Group				
Predictor	Business	Military	Government	Religion	Labor	Consumer Groups	Media	Intellectuals	Blacks	Feminists
Alienation	0.22*	0.24*	0.00	0.07*	-0.04	-0.05	0.03	-0.09*	-0.10*	0.02
Expressive individualism	0.10*	0.08*	-0.02	-0.13*	-0.04	-0.08*	-0.05	-0.09*	-0.07*	-0.06
Collective liberalism	0.20*	0.19*	-0.04	-0.10*	-0.09*	-0.04	0.02	0.11*	-0.05	0.01
Regime threat	-0.04	0.10*	0.01	-0.10*	-0.13*	-0.13*	-0.10*	-0.20*	-0.04	-0.02
R-squared	0.12*	0.16*	0.00	0.04*	0.05*	0.04*	0.01*	0.05*	0.03*	0.01

*Significant at p < 0.05.

cient). The less one thinks the regime is threatened, the more likely one is to believe that intellectuals have relatively little influence. Conversely, the more concerned one feels about threats to the regime, the more one is likely to believe that intellectuals have a great deal of power. People who are more alienated and who support the liberal position on expressive individualism also believe that blacks have relatively less power.

In short, the ideological determinants of institutional power are more complex than originally envisaged. As expected, views on business and military power are related to views on alienation and collectivist liberalism. Assessing the power of many liberal institutions (consumer groups, intellectuals, and labor) seems to be primarily a function of the regime threat dimension, as opposed to the other three ideological factors. Although ideology plays a significant role, assessing the social reality of power is clearly more than a function of ideology alone, and such assessment varies widely for different groups. The perceived power of the military and of business is the most significantly related to ideological concerns. Perceptions of other groups are not as closely tied to such concerns. As we shall see in the next section, desiring greater influence for liberal versus conservative institutions is largely a matter of ideology.

Preferred Relative Influence of Various Groups

Respondents were asked how much influence various groups ought to have. We ran a factor analysis on these responses, following the same procedure used for our factor analysis of ideology. While a factor analysis of the measures of influence rankings produces no easily interpretable set of dimensions, we find that for the measures of the groups that should have influence, two factors emerge that explain 49.6 percent of the variance.[2]

The first factor consists of the liberal groups mentioned above: feminists, black leaders, consumer groups, labor unions, intellectuals, and the media. Thus people who believe that one of these groups should have more power than it has also tend to believe that the other groups should, as well. For example, those who believe feminists should have more influence believe that other liberal groups should also have more influence. In contrast, those who think intellectuals should have less influence are more likely to think that others in this same grouping ought to have less influence.

The second factor consisted of the conservative groups: the military, business leaders, and religious leaders. Again, respondents who believe that the influence of one of these conservative groups should be higher than it is also believe the power of other conservative groups should be higher and that of the four liberal groups should be lower.

The variable "How much influence should federal government agencies have?" does not load on either factor. We discuss the results and implications of our ideological factors and increasing government influence later. We first look at the four ideological dimensions and their relationships with the liberal and conservative influence factors.

Each of the four ideological dimensions is a strong predictor of the factor "increasing the influence of liberal groups" and is statistically significant at the $p < 0.0001$ level or better (see Table 4.2). Once again, we compare the standardized coefficients to measure the importance of each ideological dimension. System alienation and collectivist liberalism are the best predictors, with standardized coefficients of 0.28 and 0.29, respectively, followed by expressive individualism and regime threat. Taken as a set, the four ideology factors explain a statistically significant 30 percent of the variance (R-squared $= 0.30$; $p < 0.05$) in the index. In contrast, self-identified ideology has an R-squared of 0.23 with the influence of liberal groups factor. The four dimensions taken together better account for elites' views on how much power liberal institutions should have than does self-reported ideology alone.

Ideology explains somewhat less of the variability of the desired influence of conservative groups. The four factors taken together explain a statistically significant 22 percent of the variance (R-squared $= 0.22$). More interestingly, regime threat, system alienation, and expressive individualism dimensions are significant predictors of the preferred influence of conservative groups. As in the first index, self-identified ideology, while a statistically significant predictor, explains only 14 percent of the variance, compared with 22 percent explained by our four dimensions of liberalism.

TABLE 4.2   Ideological Dimensions as Predictors of Preferred Power of Elite Groups (standardized regression weights)

	Standardized Regression Coefficients		
	Liberals	Conservatives	Government
System alienation	0.28*	−0.23*	0.02
Collectivist liberalism	0.29*	−0.07*	0.25*
Expressive individualism	0.14*	−0.24*	0.10*
Regime threat	0.12*	−0.22*	−0.06
R-squared	0.30*	0.22*	0.06*

N = 1,040
*Significant at p < 0.05.

Our results show a differential impact of ideology on the influence factors. Alienation and collective liberalism are the most important predictors of desired power of liberal groups, while alienation (a negative correlation), expressive individualism (a negative correlation), and regime threat (a positive correlation) are the best predictors of preferred power of conservative groups. This result indicates that the issues of importance to elites as they consider social power are different when the targets are liberal or conservative groups. It suggests that disagreements about the organization of social power may stem from disagreement about the fundamental reasons that some groups ought to have power and others not. Liberal preferences for group influence stem from the desire to improve the lot of those whom they consider to have been excluded from the system, as well as from general alienation. Conservatives, however, associate the power of such groups with a threat to the integrity of the traditional moral order.

Feelings About Government

Support for more government influence does not associate neatly with either conservatism or liberalism. The governmental variable loads weakly on both factors, and it has a complex relationship with other factors of desired influence.

In fact, separate regressions on governmental agency influence with each of the ideological factors show that only collectivist liberalism is substantially related to the desire to increase the power of government.

The data seem to point to an ambivalence both liberals and conservatives feel toward government. On the one hand, liberals appreciate the government as a means to increasing the welfare state and gay rights, and using government to promote or secure rights to or opportunities for abortion, but fear government when it involves itself in issues of crime, Communism, and other forms of threat to the existing regime. On the other hand, conservatives hate big government when it either furthers the welfare state or supports expressive lifestyle issues, but they appreciate the government when it responds to perceived internal or external threats to the system. The association with most of these variables, however, is not very strong.

TRADITIONAL VERSUS NEW CLASS GOALS AND VALUES

A second test of the general comprehensiveness of the four dimensions of ideology uses a general list of societal goals. If ideological views of elites are comprehensive and systematic, then they should not merely govern immediate policy preferences, but should strongly shape more general visions of future possibilities. One measure of such values was developed by political scientist Ronald Inglehart (1977).

Inglehart argues that the rising affluence of Western societies means that material values such as economic growth and personal security have become less important than previously. He thinks that the successful fulfillment of these material needs leads many individuals to concentrate on fulfilling their newly emerging postmaterialist concerns and thus be more responsive to attempts to fulfill postmaterialist values. Despite the doubt we have about the impact of affluence per se, and despite our skepticism regarding the psychological theory on which his argument is based, the kind of rank-ordering of materialist versus postmaterialist values required by his thesis provides a test of the generality of our measures of ideology.

We expect that liberals are more likely to choose postmaterialist values, while conservatives are more likely to choose materialist values. Ideological liberalism is closely related to Inglehart's postmaterialist values. In fact, the phraseology Inglehart uses to describe his post-materialist goals closely mirrors the language used by some leading contemporary liberals. Mario Cuomo's famous speech at the 1984 Democratic National Convention was a paean to community over individualism; Jesse Jackson's convention speech in 1988 lauded the importance of being somebody; and Hillary Rodham Clinton searches for the politics of meaning.

Rothman and Lichter used a version of Inglehart's measure that required respondents to consider what the goals of the country should be for the next ten years. Respondents were presented with a list of six goals, from which they were to select their top goal, their next highest goal, and the goal least important to them. The choices were: (1) maintaining a high rate of economic growth, (2) making sure that America has strong defense forces, (3) seeing that people have more say in how things get decided at work and in their communities, (4) progressing toward a less impersonal, more humane society, (5) fighting crime, and (6) progressing toward a society where ideas are more important than money.

Table 4.3 shows that those who think people should have more say, that America should progress toward a more humane society, or that America should favor ideas over money are much more alienated from the system than respondents who selected the goals of economic growth, strong defense, or fighting crime. Those favoring the former goals are also more supportive of collectivist liberalism than are those favoring the

TABLE 4.3   Ideological Dimensions as Predictors of Inglehart's
Materialist Goals (standardized discriminant weights)

	Mean Factor Score		
	Materialist	Postmaterialist	Standardized Weight
Alienation	96.48	103.60	0.70
Expression individualism	97.20	99.74	0.07
Collective liberalism	98.07	105.65	0.19
Regime threat	97.02	104.21	0.62

Explained variance $(1 - \text{lambda}) = 0.25$.
Chi-square $= 318.45$.
Predictors and equations are significant at $p < 0.05$.

latter goals. Lastly, supporters of postmaterialist goals see the groups that stand outside the society's moral consensus (e.g., criminals and the Soviet Union) as not constituting a serious threat to the regime, while those believing in materialist goals take the opposite view.[3]

We recoded the Inglehart goals into two categories, materialist versus postmaterialist, and ran several regressions to see which dimensions of liberalism best predict materialist versus postmaterialist goals. Since the opposition of materialist versus postmaterialist goals is a dichotomy, ordinary least squares (OLS) regression is inappropriate.[4] Instead we employed a discriminant function analysis, which, like OLS regression, builds a linear combination of the predictors to account for variability in the dependent variable. In this case, the criterion reflects group membership: advocacy of materialist or postmaterialist values. Standardized discriminant weights are interpreted similarly to regression coefficients; the larger the magnitude of the weight, the greater the influence of that predictor. When there are only two groups on the dependent measure, it is possible to calculate the explained variance for the function $(1 - \text{lambda})$, analogous to the R-squared of OLS regression. In the two-group case, discriminant analysis and OLS regression tend to yield similar results.

Although self-identified ideology performs well as a single variable, it does not predict respondent choice of materialist versus postmaterialist goals as well as do the four ideological dimensions taken together. For many purposes liberalism can be taken as a single dimensional construct, but treating ideology as multidimensional provides a more refined measure and more accurate prediction.

The discriminant function of the ideological dimensions and preference for materialist or postmaterialist goals is shown in Table 4.3. Two dimensions are strongly related to the criterion: alienation and regime threat. Collective liberalism has modest predictive value. The direction of the relationship is positive for all groups, indicating that greater liber-alism on the ideological dimensions is associated with preference for postmaterialist goals. Taken together, the four dimensions account for 25 percent of the variability in group membership (Chi-square = 318.45; $p < 0.05$).[5]

In sum, the large and consistent differences between liberals and conservatives on the Inglehart goals show that differences extend beyond questions of immediate policy issues to encompass substantial differ-ences in a larger vision of America's future. Furthermore, the four dimen-sions of ideology allow us to discern more clearly the meaning of liberal-ism and what our respondents seek for the United States. System alienation and regime threat are the two dimensions of liberalism that best predict choice of materialist versus postmaterialist values. The im-pact of the other dimensions (collectivist liberalism and expressive indi-vidualism) is minimal or nonexistent. Alienation from the system and a benign view of its moral antagonists together form the critical outlook that is most closely identified as the adversary culture.

IDEOLOGY AND JUDGING THE RELIABILITY OF THE MEDIA

Ten elite groups rated fourteen media (television, newspapers, and maga-zines) on their reliability as sources of information on public affairs.[6] Respondents rated each magazine on a scale of one to seven, where one is "not reliable" and seven is "very reliable"; they could also indicate that they did not know.

As shown in Table 4.4, sources are of two types: the television news, newspapers, and magazines; and intellectual journals of opinion. News media and magazines included the *New York Times, Time, Newsweek, U.S. News and World Report,* television network news, the Public Broad-casting System (PBS), and in some cases, the *Los Angeles Times* and the *Washington Post.*[7]

The Major Media

The more liberal respondents (as self-reported) think many of the major media outlets to be quite reliable. The news sources whose per-ceived reliability increases with increasing liberalism are: the *Washington Post* (r = 0.35), the *New York Times* (r = 0.28), PBS (r = 0.28), and television network news (r = 0.23). The news sources whose perceived reliability declines with increasing liberalism are: *U.S. News* (r = −0.37) and *Time* (r = −0.15). The relationships are statistically significant.

TABLE 4.4   Ideological Dimensions as Predictors
of Perceived Media Reliability

	Washington Post	PBS	New York Times	*Television News*	Time	U.S. News
System alienation	0.15*	0.12*	0.02	0.02	−0.15*	−0.17*
Collectivist liberalism	0.24*	0.16*	0.23*	0.24*	−0.09*	−0.14*
Expressive individualism	0.14*	0.06*	0.02	0.03	0.00	−0.14*
Regime threat	0.14*	0.08*	0.05	−0.06	−0.14*	−0.24*
R-squared	0.18*	0.08*	0.07*	0.05*	0.06*	0.21*
N	523	1,003	1,109	1,033	1,094	1,026

*Significant at $p \leq 0.05$.

Neither the *Los Angeles Times* nor *Newsweek* exhibits a statistically significant relationship with self-identified liberalism.

When we break down liberalism into four dimensions, we find all dimensions to be significantly related to the perceived reliability of most major media sources. All dimensions of liberalism are significantly ($p \leq 0.05$) related to perceptions of the *Washington Post's* reliability. The equation is statistically significant and explains 18 percent of the variance. Self-reported ideology alone explains only 13 percent of the variance.

The reliability of PBS is a function of collectivist liberalism, system alienation, and the regime threat dimensions. The equation is statistically significant ($p < 0.05$) and predicts as well as self-identified liberalism. The variables in the equation and self-identified liberalism both explain 8 percent of the variance.

The reliability rating of the *New York Times* is a function of the collectivist liberalism dimension. The remaining dimensions are not statistically significant. The equation is statistically significant ($p \leq 0.05$) and works equally well in terms of prediction compared with self-identified liberalism, accounting for 8 percent of the variability.

For television news, collectivist liberalism is the only dimension that is statistically significant ($p < 0.0001$ level). The proportion of variance explained is a statistically significant 5 percent, the same as self-identified liberalism.

The liberal underpinnings of the perceived reliability of newspapers and television news contrasts with the ideological underpinnings of reliability of the news weeklies. The perceived reliability of *Time, U.S. News and World Report,* and *Newsweek* are a function of being more conserva-

Newsweek	Los Angeles Times	National Review	New Republic	New York Review of Books	Nation	Commentary	Public Interest
−0.11*	−0.22*	−0.10	0.08*	0.15*	0.12*	−0.13*	−0.04
0.09*	0.21*	−0.13	0.14*	0.04	0.10*	−0.05	−0.19*
−0.03	−0.03	−0.26	−0.02	−0.01	0.08	−0.22*	−0.17*
−0.13*	n/a	−0.28	−0.02	0.04	−0.07	−0.19*	−0.03
0.02*	0.09*	0.28*	0.03*	0.03*	0.04*	0.15*	0.10*
1,011	208	628	707	672	546	523	313

tive on some of these dimensions, especially system alienation, and the regime threat dimension.

For *Time,* system alienation, regime threat, and expressive individualism are negatively related to perceived reliability ($p \leq 0.05$). That is, the more liberal a person is on these three dimensions, the less reliable he or she thinks *Time* to be. The overall equation is statistically significant ($p \leq 0.05$) and explains 6 percent of the variance, triple that explained by self-identified liberalism (2 percent).

Respondents who are more alienated and score low on regime threat are more likely to find *Newsweek* unreliable. None of the other dimensions is statistically significant. The overall equation only explains 2 percent of the variance. Self-identified liberalism is not statistically significant.

The *Los Angeles Times* results are puzzling at first sight. In the regression equation, both system alienation and collectivist liberalism are statistically significant, but they are significant in the opposite directions. The more alienated a respondent is, the less he or she is likely to consider the *Los Angeles Times* reliable, while the more collectivist liberal a respondent is, the more reliable he or she finds the *Los Angeles Times.* However, we do know that these variables measure different aspects of liberalism. One can strongly support collectivist liberalism and yet not be alienated, and vice versa.[8]

For *U.S. News,* every dimension of liberalism is inversely related to perceived reliability. Regime threat has the largest standardized regression coefficient, followed by nearly identical scores for collectivist liberalism, system alienation, and expressive individualism. This means that those who see little threat to the regime view *U.S. News* as unreliable. The overall equation is statistically significant and explains 21 percent of the variance. In contrast, self-identified liberalism explains only 14 percent of the variance.

U.S. News stands out from the other journals for what we consider obvious reasons: it is the only mass circulation journal that self-consciously identifies itself as conservative and is more readily perceived as being conservative by those who read it as well as those who do not.

Intellectual Journals

The ideological patterns related to perceived reliability of these journals are similar to those of the major media outlets. Although not all our respondents are familiar with all of these journals, the importance of these intellectual journals for shaping the public debate on many issues is incontestable.[9] The extent to which our respondents feel able to comment about them either positively or negatively is a further indication of the depth and sophistication of their ideological views. We asked respondents to judge the reliability of six intellectual journals: the *National Review*, the *New Republic*, the *New York Review of Books*, the *Nation*, *Commentary*, and the *Public Interest*.

Many respondents claimed not to know the reliability of some of the journals. For the *National Review*, 41 percent responded "don't know"; the *New Republic*, 35 percent; the *New York Review of Books*, 36 percent; the *Nation*, 48 percent; *Commentary*, 51 percent; and the *Public Interest*, 72 percent. In each case, we found that the proportion of "don't knows" increased as we moved closer to the center of the political spectrum. Those on the ends of the political spectrum, the more extreme conservatives and liberals, have opinions, positive and negative, about the journals. Stated somewhat differently, there is a nonlinear (quadratic) relationship between giving a "don't know" response and political ideology. This is probably the case because such persons are more sensitive to the issues and more highly motivated to determine the ideological framework within which such journals operate. The remainder of the analysis eliminates the "don't knows" by combining them with other cases with missing data and thus omitting them.[10]

As expected, self-identified ideology is related to the perceived reliability of a journal, and all results are statistically significant. The correlations are as follows: the *National Review*, $r = -0.42$; the *New Republic*, $r = 0.12$; the *New York Review of Books*, $r = 0.15$; the *Nation*, $r = 0.19$; *Commentary*, $r = -0.26$; the *Public Interest*, $r = -0.21$. The more conservative think that the *National Review, Commentary,* and the *Public Interest* are more reliable, while the more liberal believe that the *New Republic,* the *New York Review of Books,* and the *Nation* are more reliable sources of information.

For the *National Review,* three dimensions (collectivist liberalism, expressive individualism, and regime threat) are predictors of reliability. The equation is statistically significant ($p \leq 0.05$) and explains 28 percent of the variance. Thus it is a far better predictor than is self-identified ideology (R-squared $= 0.17$).

For the *New Republic,* a more centrist journal, we find a much weaker prediction. Only system alienation and collectivist liberalism are statistically significant, and the proportion of variance explained by them is small. For both the *New York Review of Books* and the *Nation,* system alienation is the most significant explanatory factor. The fact that greater system alienation increases one's perceptions of reliability of these two left journals demonstrates the importance of the post-1960s adversary culture for the evaluation of these journals.

Collectivist liberalism and expressive individualism relate inversely to the perceived reliability of the *Public Interest.* The R-squared is higher for the equations containing the four dimensions of liberalism (R-squared $= 0.10$) than for self-identified liberalism (R-squared $= 0.04$).

For *Commentary,* three dimensions of liberalism are statistically significant; the exception is collectivist liberalism. A factor composed of the other three dimensions is statistically significant and is higher (R-squared $= 0.15$) than that for self-identified liberalism alone (R-squared $= 0.07$). This statistical evidence supports the contention that *Commentary* is the magazine of neoconservatism. Many neoconservatives accept the welfare state, hence the lack of a relationship between collectivist liberalism and reliability for this journal. *Commentary,* however, criticizes modern liberalism for its alienation and expressive individualism, as well as, in the mid-1980s, for its foreign policy preferences. The negative relationship between scores on regime threat, expressive individualism, and system alienation and the perceived reliability of the magazine may reflect this orientation.

Ideology, defined as part of a comprehensive worldview, thus colors how we assess the quality of the information we receive. Ideology, whether measured as self-labeled ideology or attitudinal dimensions, influences the perceived reliability of some news outlets and opinion journals. In cases where liberalism significantly predicts reliability, the four dimensions of liberalism taken as a set consistently outperforms self-identified liberalism.

IDEOLOGY AND VOTING

In addition, elites were asked about their votes for president. Media and business leaders were asked about every election from 1964 to 1976, while the other elite groups were asked about each election from 1968 to 1980.[11] We computed discriminant functions for each election separately. Each vote variable was recorded so that a value of one was assigned to the Democratic candidate and a value of two was assigned to the Republican candidate.[12]

The results of the analysis are presented in Table 4.5. For the 1964 election, the results do not include the regime threat dimension, as they were not available for business and the media. Collectivist liberalism and expressive individualism, much more than system alienation, are related to partisan voting, though all three dimensions contribute to explaining the variance of the dependent variable.

In the 1964 election, all three factors influenced voting in the expected direction, explaining 15 percent of the variance. In 1968, all four factors exhibited explanatory power, though collectivist liberalism was the most significant. Taken together, the ideological factors accounted for 40 percent of the variability in the dependent measure. In 1972 the most important predictor was system alienation—explained, we think, by the character of the candidates. Nevertheless, all four factors played a role, accounting jointly for almost half of the variance. Essentially the same patterns characterize the 1976 and 1980 elections, with system alienation in 1976 and regime threat in 1980 as the most important factors. All four dimensions, however, are predictors and they jointly explain 56 percent of the variance.

Two points are clear. First, all ideological dimensions are important

TABLE 4.5   Ideological Dimensions as Predictors of Voting, 1964–80 (discriminant function weights)

	1964	1968	1972	1976	1980
System alienation	0.26	−0.39	−0.54	0.56	0.49
Collectivist liberalism	0.81	0.58	0.48	−0.51	−0.51
Expressive individualism	0.50	0.41	0.48	−0.33	−0.39
Regime threat		0.42	0.45	−0.36	−0.54
Explained variance (1 − lambda)	0.15	0.40	0.49	0.36	0.56
N	332	889	980	1,041	877

All equations and predictors are significant at $p < 0.05$.
Note: 1 = Democrat; 2 = Republican

predictors of voting. For the most part these dimensions explain far more of the variance than does self-identified liberalism. Interestingly, the separate dimensions taken together predict the two most ideological elections, 1972 and 1980, best of all. Second, there seems to be a rising undercurrent of discontent with the American system among elite Democratic supporters. System alienation becomes a significant factor after the 1968 election, and remains so. One suspects that a study today would find it playing an even more significant role.

SUMMARY AND CONCLUSION

Elite political ideology matters. Political liberalism has a large impact on respondents' perceptions of the influence of institutions, observed as well as desired, broad-gauged, long-term societal goals, the perceived reliabilities of a variety of news media and opinion magazines, and voting behavior. The findings support our view that contemporary ideology is a powerful cultural system, producing distinctive and antagonistic worldviews, liberalism and conservatism, that encompass much of social, economic, and political life.

We also find that measuring ideology as a four-dimensional construct provides two kinds of superiority over relying on self-identified ideology on a conservative to liberal scale. First, the four dimensional construct items generally predict better than self-identified ideology. Among perceived influence rankings of various groups, the composite predicts better in eight out of ten cases. For the two desired influence factors, the composite predicts considerably better than does self-identified ideology. The composite predicted respondent's choice of top goals better, as well as many of the reliabilities of news sources. Even for voting, except for the 1964 election, the combinations of liberalism dimensions predicted better than did self-identified ideology.

The second kind of superiority of the combination of ideological factors is more important than sheer predictive power. Self-identified ideology by itself gives no indication of what the term means to our respondents. Use of the separate dimensions allows us to understand which aspect of liberalism or conservatism is important in any given case by permitting us to specify the meanings of the relationships more precisely. This allows us to draw certain conclusions unavailable from a simple measure of ideology.

Collectivist liberalism, the dimension most highly correlated with self-identified liberalism, is not always the best predictor variable: system alienation, regime threat, and expressive individualism are on many occasions as good or better predictors. While traditional economic issues continue to play an important role in American life, it is clear that certain cultural issues have become increasingly important.

Our results allow us to advance a tentative hypothesis: namely, that the notion of the adversary culture is best reflected in a combination of system alienation and regime threat. To be against the system is to regard it as fundamentally flawed (system alienation), and to be against the system is to take lightly, or even welcome, moral challenges to its existence (regime threat). Thus we found that the system alienation and regime threat dimensions each predicts choice of postmaterialist goals better than does collectivist liberalism, and system alienation predicts ratings of both the *Nation* and the *New York Review of Books*, the premier journals of alienated intellectuals, better than does collectivist liberalism.

FIVE

THE COMPONENTS OF COLLECTIVIST LIBERALISM

The history of the modern American intellectual class is also the history of the idea of collectivist liberalism, or what is often called liberal progressivism.[1] Intellectuals and academics before the Progressive era embraced no single paradigm, but many incorporated some form of laissez-faire individualism. In journalism, E. L. Godkin's *Nation* argued for both clean government and classical liberalism, complete with laissez-faire economics (Goldman, 1952; Fine, 1956). In sociology, Herbert Spencer and later William Graham Sumner made the case for laissez-faire individualism and the survival of the fittest, while arguing the folly of most social reform.[2] In political science John W. Burgess, organizer of Columbia University's faculty of political science, taught the value of limited government to students that included A. Lawrence Lowell and Nicholas Murray Butler—future presidents of Harvard and Columbia universities (Fine, 1956, pp. 91–95). In law, Justice Stephen Field and other orthodox legal scholars prescribed constitutional interpretation supporting laissez-faire capitalism; in economics, Francis Bowen, Laurence Laughlin, Amasa Walker, and Simon Newcomb extended the principles of classical economic theory (ibid., p. 48).

In education, William Torrey Harris spoke in favor of free enterprise and the necessity of preserving private property as a force in maintaining the level of civilization (Curti, 1959).[3] As the founder of the philosophical school known as St. Louis Hegelians, the editor of the *Journal of Speculative Philosophy,* the superintendent of St. Louis's schools, the U.S. commissioner of education, and a member of the National Educational Association's Committee of Ten, Harris disparaged the necessity of manual training in schools, arguing that the purpose of education at all levels was to transmit the heritage of Western civilization (Curti, 1959, pp. 310–47; Hirsch, 1987, pp. 116–17; Ravitch, 1983, pp. 71–72, 119–20, 137–43; Cremin, 1988, pp. 157–64).[4]

History as an academic discipline had its own classical liberal scholars, but their works have been likewise disparaged by modern historians, most notably Richard Hofstadter (1970, pp. 25–29). They include such figures as James Ford Rhodes, a significant contributor to the now-standard abolitionist interpretation of the Civil War. Rhodes today would clearly be called a conservative, or in Rhodes's own words, "one inclined towards individualism," who recognized the permanence of the debate between socialism and individualism (Rhodes, 1928, vol. 9, pp. 166, 165).

Beginning with the 1890s, the intellectual revolt began in earnest with results so pervasive that only the names of the innovators need be mentioned. In sociology, the work of Lester Frank Ward and Albion Small decisively eclipsed Sumner's in popularity. In history, Charles A. Beard, Carl Becker, and V. L. Parrington emerged as the leading historians of the day (Hofstadter, 1970). In philosophy, pragmatism, especially the thought of John Dewey, became what many came to call the national philosophy. In economics, Thorstein Veblen became the foremost institutionalist critic of neoclassical economics. In law, Supreme Court Justice Oliver Wendell Holmes declared that the U.S. Constitution does not assume Herbert Spencer's *Social Statics*. In journalism, Herbert Croly's *New Republic* became the most important magazine for the progressive intelligentsia. (On all of these thinkers, see White, 1949; Goldman, 1952; Forcey, 1961; and Fine, 1956.)[5]

As early as 1909, Croly himself foresaw the nationalizing and socializing aspect of progressive reform. Croly's beliefs, in amplified, expanded, and deepened form, provide the basis for modern-day collectivist liberalism, first as the basis of Theodore Roosevelt's New Nationalism and later through Croly's editorship of the *New Republic* (Goldman, 1952).

Croly sketched out the task for liberals as the pursuit of Jeffersonian ends by Hamiltonian means. He argued that Jefferson "sought an essentially equalitarian and even socialistic result by means of an essentially individualistic machinery" (Croly, 1965 [orig. 1909], p. 43)—a formula inherently doomed to failure. Especially at fault was the widespread acceptance of the slogan "equal rights for all, special privileges for none." Croly thought this formula, one even "predatory millionaires could accept," legitimized the status quo, and defeated all reform aspirations (pp. 148–54, esp. pp. 150–51). He concluded that Jeffersonian individualism must be abandoned "for the benefit of a genuinely individual and social consummation; naive reformers do not realize how dangerous and fallacious a chart their cherished principle of equal rights may well become" (p. 153).[6]

It was Alexander Hamilton who sought the "energetic and intelligent assertion of the national good" (Croly, 1965, p. 45) and supplied the indispensable means toward Jeffersonian ends. Of course, "Hamiltonianism must be transformed into a thoroughly democratic political principle" (p. 153). By this, Croly means that the majority should come to direct spheres of life that Jefferson, Hamilton, and the American people long assumed to be the individual's responsibility. "Popular government is to make itself expressly and permanently responsible for the amelioration of the individual and society; and a necessary consequence is an adequate organization and reconstructive policy" (p. 209).

The liberal-progressive revolt was not all of a piece. Moderates believed that the system could be made to live up to its own promises and suggested specific institutional reforms. Radicals believed that the system required fundamental structural change. For example, Ida Tarbell and Henry Demarest Lloyd were both critics of John D. Rockefeller's Standard Oil Corporation. Tarbell was a moderate, however, and eventually became an advocate of big business capitalism. Lloyd, in contrast, was a crusading journalist and advocated a "cooperative commonwealth"; by the end of his life he was a supporter of Eugene Debs's Socialist party. Similarly, one can distinguish between reformer Henry George's *Progress and Poverty,* which envisioned his single tax on land correcting an otherwise healthy capitalistic economic system, and radical Edward Bellamy's *Looking Backwards,* which described a future society where a socialist utopia was fully established. Moderates were initially more prominent, and argued that the full potential of the American system could be achieved or restored by a series of ad hoc institutional reforms: the Pendleton Act (civil service reform), the single tax, the Sherman Antitrust Act, a bimetallic currency (e.g., gold and the election of 1896), lower tariffs, and avid trust bursting. Influential from the turn of the century until World War I, the programs of the moderate reformers were submerged into Woodrow Wilson's New Freedoms, Teddy Roosevelt's New Nationalism, and later reemerged piecemeal with the New Deal's trust-busting phase. Their influence has remained a permanent, albeit diminishing, part of liberalism.

Members of the radical branch, the American equivalent of the British Fabian Socialists, believed that the defects of the capitalist system were so great that their remedy entailed fundamental change. Many of these intellectuals ended up supporting one form or another of democratic socialism. Although marginal at first, the radicals acquired more influence with the New Nationalism of Roosevelt and Herbert Croly (author of *The Promise of American Life*). The experience of World War I's "war socialism" provided an experiential basis for further social reform in this direction (e.g., Higgs, 1987). Radical influence pervaded the New Deal's quasi corporatism and, as an economic policy, provided the core of what we call collectivist liberalism (Lerner, Nagai, and Rothman, 1990b).

According to leading liberal historian Arthur Schlesinger, Jr., the New Deal completed the exorcism of Jeffersonian inhibitions regarding strong government, committing liberals ever after to the Hamiltonian–Theodore Roosevelt faith in the state as the instrument of social welfare (Schlesinger, 1988 [orig. 1949], p. 181). Despite the brief interregnum in its political influence during the 1920s, the collectivist liberalism, reformist-oriented "synthesis" became dominant among American intellectuals during the Great Depression. By 1950, Lionel Trilling could write that liberal ideas were the only ideas in circulation. Arthur Schlesinger, Jr., could assume that only progressives create our contemporary climate of opinion, and historian George Nash could conclude that the conservative intellectual movement had reached the nadir of its influence (Trilling, 1950; Schlesinger, 1988, p. 35; Nash, 1976).

In what might be called a charter statement for future activities of the American intellectual class, philosopher William James writes of an intellectual aristocracy "which corresponds to that of older countries": "We ought to have our own class consciousness. 'Les Intellectuals!' What prouder clubname could there be than this one," which refers to those "who still retained some critical sense and judgment" (1971 [orig. 1907], pp. 21–22). As to where this sense leads, James confesses, "My own utopia . . . [is] in the reign of peace and in the gradual advent of some sort of socialistic equilibrium" (p. 11).

James's pragmatist colleague John Dewey, however, was a more consistent and explicit democratic socialist, coining the term *collectivistic liberalism*. Taking into account the political realities of the times, Dewey writes of how anything labeled as socialism would be seriously handicapped—"But in the long run, the realities of the situation will exercise control over the connotations which, for historical reasons, cling to a word" (1930, p. 104).

COLLECTIVIST LIBERALISM AND SOCIAL CHANGE: THE WORKS OF JOHN DEWEY

John Dewey's writings embody better than any other the links connecting collectivist liberalism and post–New Deal efforts at social reform. Dewey always believed in democracy and in intelligence and experiment as a means of solving social problems. He appealed to intellectuals to unite in a movement that sought a "consciously directed critical consideration of the state of society" (1930, pp. 138–42), and he claimed that such union would help them "to recover their social function [of social criticism] and refind themselves" (pp. 138–42).

Believing that an individualistic, competitive, and capitalistic America was radically and fundamentally defective, Dewey argued that it should be (and inevitably would be) replaced by some form of democratic socialism, albeit gradually and without violence.[7] Most important, he believed that education would be the primary means for collectivistic progress and social reform.

Dewey thought democratic socialism was the only way to achieve a true individuality and at the same time a true community (e.g., *Individualism Old and New,* 1930; *Liberalism and Social Action,* 1935). He writes, apropos of Lockean liberalism and laissez-faire capitalism: "The course of historic events has proved they emancipated the classes whose special interests they represented, rather than human beings impartially. . . . Fortunately it is not necessary to attempt the citation of relevant facts. Practically everyone admits there is a new social problem . . . and that these problems have an economic basis" (1960, p. 271).[8]

On the question of socialism itself, philosopher Sidney Hook, perhaps Dewey's closest disciple, provides a good critique. He admits in his autobiography that "for all our scientific outlook we were not empirical enough. We accepted the quasi-mystical outlook in assuming the social and economic forces determined the future for which we had no moral role or responsibility" (1987, p. 525). He also states that Dewey, along with Hook and others, were "intensely interested in the economic questions of the day," but knew nothing about economics (p. 599). Their ignorance of economics is reflected in Hook's comment that "Socialists— and I include myself among them—never took the problem of incentives seriously in the socialized sector of the economy" (p. 601). Conventional neoclassical economics would have taught them that removing incentives results in "a decline in productivity, an erosion in the skills of craftsmanship, and in the work ethic" (p. 601).

Such comments regarding socialism did not require historical hindsight. Several thinkers of the 1930s, including economist Harry Gideonse and journalist Walter Lippmann, made these arguments frequently and cogently. Nonetheless, Dewey, Beard, and other collectivist liberal intellectuals agreed with Anne Morrow Lindberg's memorable statement that collectivism was the wave of the future and there was no use fighting it (1940, p. 37). To further the inevitable, Dewey, along with Beard and others, thought the American school system should be used as a mechanism to promote this appropriate social change.

Writing American history from a left-liberal slant flowed inevitably from collectivist liberalism in American intellectual life. Dewey was not unique among intellectuals eagerly awaiting capitalism's inevitable demise. Historian Charles Beard was a staunch proponent of "economic planning and an admirer of the nationalism of the early New Deal," and his nationalist collectivism found expression in policies he outlined for the development of social studies in American schools (Ekirch, 1969, pp. 129, 131). Convinced that capitalism was doomed and a new age of collectivism was on the horizon, Beard believed that teaching a doctrine of individualism would lead to an "increase in the accompanying social tensions" (ibid., p. 131). Education had to be adjusted to meet modern needs.[9]

By 1950, the cultural transformation was complete. Thus historian Samuel E. Morison could write:

> Fifty years ago, it was difficult to find any general history of the United States that did not present the Federalist-Whig-Republican point of view, or express a dim view of all Democratic leaders except Cleveland. This fashion has completely changed; it would be equally difficult today to find a good general history of the United States that did not follow the Jefferson-Jackson-F. D. Roosevelt line. (1951, p. 272)

Collectivist liberalism, however, would not have spread far beyond a small circle of intellectuals and academics had it not been for the Great Depression. As Geertz (1973) points out, new ideologies emerge when the old culture cannot provide a template for new events. This view explains the relationship between intellectuals' writings on collectivist liberalism and their eventual simplification and transformation into a significant dimension of popular American ideology. Collectivist liberalism, as part of the post–New Deal ideology, emerged because American charity and the American private sector could not cope with the economic crisis of the Depression.

THE CRISIS OF AMERICAN CHARITY AND THE RISE OF A NEW AMERICAN IDEOLOGY

The era of Harding, Coolidge, and Hoover is seen as one of political conservatism. This was also the period when intellectuals, colleges, academics, foundation managers, and civil servants started a network between foundations, nonprofit organizations, and government, culminating in President Hoover's government-foundation collaboration, *Report on Recent Social Trends* (Hofstadter, 1948; Coben, 1991). During this period academics and foundations developed survey research as a vehicle for social reform. For furthering social policy, the Social Science Research Council, the National Bureau of Economic Research, and the first think-tank (the Brookings Institute) were formed (Karl and Katz, 1981, pp. 266–67).

The Depression, however, was the major turning point for government intervention in the economic sphere. Private charity could not meet the crisis of the time. Hoover engaged in extensive efforts to stimulate private, state, and local nonprofit activity, and, consistent with his philosophy, limited the federal government while encouraging private charity to meet public needs. The American Red Cross even spurned a proposed congressional grant of twenty-five million dollars and undertook a relief effort with five million from its general campaign and an additional fifteen million from a special campaign (Bremner, 1988, p. 138).

In 1931, Hoover planned and carried out a major national campaign, the Organization for Unemployment Relief, which raised over one hundred million dollars from both local and private sources of charity. As the crisis deepened, Hoover, with congressional authorization of the Reconstruction Finance Corporation, gradually shifted toward the kind of central government involvement characteristic of the New Deal, but without Roosevelt's enthusiasm for collective action and resulting political success.

The literature on the government's response to the Depression is so vast that even to summarize it would take more space than we have available (see Sitkoff, 1985, for bibliographies; McCraw's 1985 essay on New Deal economic policy; Bremner [1988] on social welfare policies). Hoover's policies, with their stress on morale and morality, contrasted radically with Roosevelt's optimism. Roosevelt did not make the political mistakes of his predecessors, but based his New Deal policies on the "common man" and "the forgotten man" (ironically, a phrase coined by

William Graham Sumner, a principal advocate of rugged individualism). Roosevelt and his New Deal—for political scientists the very model of a modern critical realignment—quite successfully and apparently permanently remolded American politics.

The ideological worldview of collectivist liberalism that justified substantial federal control over economic policy, substantial redistribution of income, and the emergence and expansion of the welfare state came from the academic and intellectual classes. The Great Depression was the historical event that fundamentally challenged popular notions of American liberal capitalism and incorporated an alternative vision as a permanent part of the American political culture. The writings of Croly, Beard, and Dewey are significantly more complex than the cluster of positions associated with support for welfare-state liberalism; nevertheless, they are the intellectual bedrock from which this strand of American liberalism developed.[10]

The prominence of collectivist liberalism as part of the Democratic agenda since the New Deal means that belief in collectivist liberalism is most closely associated with labor. Moreover, since it became a significant issue when the elites in the survey were young (median age of sample is forty-six), we expect to find that collectivist liberalism is an important part of the liberalism passed down from parent to child.

DATA ANALYSIS OF COLLECTIVIST LIBERALISM

Labor leaders are a liberal group; almost three of four define themselves as liberal. This indicates they are as liberal as the leading creators of television and film (75 and 67 percent, respectively), and more liberal than the media elite (55 percent). Public interest group leaders are the only elite group in which a larger number of respondents define themselves as liberals (91 percent).[11]

An overwhelming majority of labor leaders have been consistent supporters of Democrats, even during the debacle of the 1972 election. In 1968, 88 percent of the two-party vote of labor leaders went to Humphrey. In 1972, the percentage of their Democratic vote declined to 78 percent. In 1976, the percentage was 90 percent and has remained at that level.

Nevertheless, reliance on political self-identification and even voting records for ideological labeling can be misleading, since similar labels can conceal wide differences in opinion. Our data show that labor leaders are not uniformly liberal on all issues, but they are one of the most liberal elite groups on collectivist liberalism. This profile is highlighted when we compare labor's views on these issues with those of the cultural elites (journalists, filmmakers, and television makers) and public interest leaders.

As Table 5.1 shows, the only issue on which a majority of labor, media, film, television, and public interest elites agree is on government's role in reducing the income gap. On all others, there is a disparity between labor and cultural elites. For example, only 35 percent of labor leaders and fewer than one in five of the public interest elite think less regulation of business is good, while a majority of cultural elites favor less government regulation of business.

Most labor leaders and the public interest elite think government should guarantee jobs, while a majority of the cultural elite think government should not. Labor, however, diverges somewhat from other liberal elites on the environment. Most leaders in trade unions, the media, movies, television, and public interest groups think environmental problems are serious (Table 5.1 does not show the intensity of that belief). Cultural elites and the public interest leaders, however, feel much more intensely than trade union leaders that environmental problems are serious. Forty-eight percent of trade union leaders strongly believe that environmental problems are serious. This compares to 55 percent of journalists, 61 percent of movie elites, 62 percent of television elites, and 81 percent of public interest leaders.

General consensus among liberal elites is reflected in their collectivist liberalism scores (see Table 3.3). Trade union and public interest group leaders rate highest on this factor. Labor's collectivist liberalism score is 105.07, slightly less liberal than public interest leaders (109.91).

TABLE 5.1   Elite Attitudes Regarding Collectivist Liberalism:
Labor Versus New Elites (percentage agree)

	Labor	Media	Movies	Television	Public Interest
Less government regulation of business is good	35	63	50	65	18
Government should not guarantee jobs	35	52	62	55	20
Environmental problems are not as serious as people have been led to believe	23	18	18	14	5
Government should reduce the income gap	70	67	60	65	94
N	95	238	96	104	158

Both are more liberal than cultural elites (media, movie, and television), whose scores range around 100.

One more issue points to the strong commitment in this area by both trade union and public interest group leaders. Elites were asked whether the more able should earn more. This question did not load on the factor analysis, and large majorities of all elites think greater ability should yield more pay. However, public interest group leaders are somewhat more egalitarian than other groups. Only 26 percent of such leaders strongly agree that the more able should earn more, compared with 46 percent of trade union leaders, 49 percent of journalists, 65 percent of filmmakers, and 68 percent of business leaders.

Irving Kristol (1978) argues that these differences in collectivist liberalism suggest the new class (or what we call new strategic elites) is anticapitalism and antibusiness; our data show the picture to be more mixed. Except for public interest leaders, labor is more liberal on these issues than are the new strategic elites. The liberalism and adversarial stand taken by many members of new strategic elites is not based on only their economic antipathy toward business. As we discuss in chapter seven, the political ideology of new strategic elites is an ideological break with the past. Their adversarial posture does not draw from the collectivist liberalism associated with the New Deal and later the Great Society, but is composed of a different view entirely. They dislike business because they associate it with the inhibitions and, as they see it, the corruptions of bourgeois society.

If the liberalism associated with new strategic elites is radically different from that of the past, parental influence on political values should be strongest in relation to collectivist liberalism and weakest on the post-1960s issues of expressive individualism (abortion and gay rights).

THE FAMILY'S INFLUENCE ON POLITICAL VALUES

High scores on collectivist liberalism are characteristic of all elites who regard themselves as liberal. Labor, a traditionally liberal elite, and liberal new strategic elites—public interest leaders, journalists, the movie elite, and makers of prime-time television—all share values that support an activist welfare state. To what extent are all these liberal members of strategic elites shaped by their family backgrounds? Were their parents politically active? Were they liberal?

Because American ideology is composed of four separate dimensions, does political socialization differ for each dimension? Parental influence should be the strongest on our elites' views of collectivist liberalism, which is a product of the New Deal era. The characteristic new class sensibility, however, is reflected in issues of system alienation, expressive individualism, and regime threat. On these issues, parental influence should be the weakest.

Measuring Parental Views

Respondents rated their parents' political views on the same seven-point used for self-identified political ideology. Respondents rated separately their fathers' political views and their mothers' political views; mothers and fathers were also rated separately. This approach presents both an opportunity and a problem. We can compare the influence of each parent on political ideology. For example, we can ask, is the influence of both parents positive, but the fathers' influence somewhat greater than the mothers' influence, because our elites were brought up with the notion that politics is a "masculine" sphere of activity? Alternatively, mothers may have been more successful than fathers in transmitting their views to offspring, since they probably spent more time with them. Jennings and Niemi (1981) find this to be true among the general public.

The problem with entering both variables into the same equation is that the resulting multicollinearity would understate their true influence, as mothers' and fathers' political views are highly correlated ($r =$ 0.63). The possible ways to treat the problem are to analyze both mothers' and fathers' views separately, or to combine them into indexes. We tried both methods, but decided to treat fathers' and mothers' views as separate variables, in separate regression equations. The general findings are the same for both parents' views on the ideological dimensions. Here we discuss the impact of parents' views on current beliefs relying on the regression equations using fathers' views.[12]

To measure respondents' political ideology, we relied on the factor scores for the four ideological dimensions (Table 5.2). The zero-order

TABLE 5.2   Ideological Dimensions and Parental Ideology (correlation coefficients)

	System Alienation	Expressive Individualism	Collective Liberalism	Regime Threat
Father's view	0.16*	0.10*	0.26*	0.18*
N	(1,726)	(1,726)	(1,726)	(1,081)
Mother's view	0.13*	0.12*	0.24*	0.18*
N	(1,742)	(1,742)	(1,742)	(1,084)

*Significant at $p < 0.05$.

results support the notion that fathers' and mothers' views are each positively related to most current political views. Though the correlations are modest, the ideological direction corresponds with our expectations. Consistent with our expectations, too, mothers' and fathers' views are most highly correlated with respondents' views on collectivist liberalism.

The relationship between parents' political liberalism and current views on collectivist liberalism, however, could be due to the social background in which the respondent grew up. Current political views on collectivist liberalism, then, would be a product of occupation and lifestyle. If this is so, then the relation between fathers' political views and current views on collectivism should vanish when we control for social background.

What if current political values are learned primarily from one's parents and are not the simple reflection and by-product of one's social background? In this case, parental views would have a statistically significant, independent effect on collectivist liberalism, separate from (i.e., controlling for) social variables. To determine the relationship between parental ideology and respondents' political beliefs, we controlled for respondents' current occupation and various background variables, including, among others, race, sex, age, socioeconomic status of family of origin, and respondents' education (see Table 5.3).[13]

Taken in conjunction with our earlier findings, parental views have considerable influence on respondents' views on collectivist liberalism, even when we controlled for social variables such as race, sex, occupation, education, and whether or not the respondent is Jewish. Parents' values also have some influence on respondents' views on perceptions of regime threat, but less on feelings of system alienation. Parental attitudes have little or no impact on respondents' views toward issues of expressive individualism.

In addition, the social background variables, especially those associated with one's family of origin, have little to do with one's current political views. We added father's occupational level, father's income, and father's educational level. These variables are not correlated with any of the ideological dimensions, nor do they have an effect on the relationship between parents' views and the respondent's ideology. (This analysis is not displayed in tabular form.)

DISCUSSION AND CONCLUSION

We have shown that American elites disagree on many issues. Consistent with the idea of multiple and conflicted strategic elites in postindustrial

TABLE 5.3   Relative Influence of Parent's Ideology on Respondent's Ideology (standardized regression weights)

	Criterion			
Predictor	System Alienation	Collective Liberalism	Expressive Individualism	Regime Threat
Father's view	0.06*	0.14*	0.03	0.11*
Occupation				
Bureaucrats	−0.15*	−0.02	−0.19*	−0.24*
Business	−0.16*	−0.19*	−0.23*	n/a
Congressional aides	−0.11*	−0.02	−0.18*	−0.24*
Judges	−0.17*	0.03	−0.20*	−0.07*
Labor	0.02	0.12*	−0.16*	−0.19*
Lawyers	−0.24*	−0.04	−0.08*	−0.12*
Media	−0.07*	0.07*	−0.02	n/a
Military	−0.17*	−0.13*	−0.36*	−0.49*
Movies	0.05	0.01	0.00	n/a
Public interest	0.12*	0.22*	−0.05	−0.09*
Religious leaders	−0.01	0.13*	−0.43*	n/a
Race	0.14*	0.03	0.03	−0.01
Sex	0.10*	0.02	0.14*	0.05
Jewish	−0.06*	−0.11	−0.13*	0.00
Education	−0.09*	0.08*	0.07*	0.11*
R-squared	0.22*	0.24*	0.29*	0.24*
Change in R-squared	0.00028	0.0153	0.0007	0.0107

*Significant at $p < 0.05$.
Change in R-squared indicates the increase in the explanatory power of the equation with the addition of father's view.

society, current occupation remains the most powerful predictor of political attitudes. Controlling for current occupation and a host of other background variables, several of which are significant in their own right, fathers' views and mothers' views do appear to influence respondents' beliefs concerning regime threat, collectivist liberalism, and to a lesser degree system alienation. Parental views do not have any significant impact on our respondents' views with regard to expressive individualism.

In other words, parental views at least moderately shape respondents' outlooks on collectivist liberalism. Issues grouped under the rubric of expressive individualism, such as abortion and homosexuality, were not controversial subjects at the time many of our respondents came of age. It is unlikely that they extensively discussed such matters as the pros and cons of adultery or abortion with their children (our elites), thus decreasing the likelihood of their influencing our respondents.

The positive results found for parental influence on collectivist liberalism are consistent with this explanation as well. We hypothesize that, at the time of the New Deal, the central political issues concerned the appropriate extent of government regulation of the economy, the desirable degree of income redistribution by the government, and the propriety of government funding of social welfare programs, that is, collectivist liberalism. Since many of our elites probably became aware of politics during the 1930s and 1940s families who talked about politics frequently would have discussed New Deal issues; under these conditions parents' attitudes toward collectivist liberalism would have been passed down to the children.

These historical effects may well include self-identified liberalism also, partly because self-identification correlates more highly with collectivist liberalism ($r = 0.60$) than with either system alienation ($r = 0.41$) or expressive individualism ($r = 0.34$). Our respondents appear to associate the labels "liberal" and "conservative" more with their positions on collectivist liberalism than with issues of system alienation or expressive individualism, though we should keep in mind that self-identification is the complex result of all the ideological dimensions. We would also speculate that parental liberalism predicts the self-identified liberalism of children better than any of the other measures of liberalism because of how political ideology is learned. Ideology is probably learned en bloc, not by stringing together various issue positions and then deciding that one is a liberal or a conservative. More likely, a person discovers that he or she is a liberal or conservative before having a clear idea of exactly what that means in terms of issue positions. This could also account for why persons remain liberal (or conservative) despite the fact that the content of such positions shifts over time. We did find greater continuity for alienation and regime threat than we had expected, however, possibly because it represents an underlying psychological predisposition toward established institutions as much as attitudes on any particular issue.

Thus the mixed effects of parental socialization on elite ideology are consistent with the strength of occupational effects. New strategic occupations were ideologically most like labor, a traditional liberal elite on issues of collectivist liberalism. Traditional elites such as business, the military, and labor are significantly more conservative than new strategic elites on issues of expressive individualism and regime threat dimensions, precisely those issues where parental influence on our elites is the weakest.

SIX

EXPRESSIVE INDIVIDUALISM, RELIGION, AND THE FAMILY

Many issues associated with the dimension of Puritan restraint versus expressive individualism are among the most divisive issues in modern American life. William Bennett—noted intellectual, former chairman of the National Endowment for the Humanities under Ronald Reagan, and secretary of education under George Bush—writes:

> Many of us lost confidence in our right and our duty to affirm publicly the desirability of what most of us believe privately. . . . We ceased being clear about the standards which we hold and the principles by which we judge, or, if we were clear in our own minds, we somehow abdicated the area of public discussion and institutional decision making to those who challenged our traditional values. As a result, we suffered a cultural breakdown of sorts—in areas like education, family life, crime and drug use, as well as in our attitudes toward sex, individual responsibility, civic duty, and public service. (1992, p. 33)

Such words are not mere rhetoric. As President Clinton discovered, the search for a compromise policy on these lifestyle issues dramatically increases, not decreases, the conflict over American values. The tenor of the arguments advanced by cultural conservatives and cultural liberals highlights the extent to which the right and the left feel under siege.

American elites, especially those in the cultural sphere, simultaneously shape and reflect the debate current in the larger society. In this chapter, we demonstrate that what has been called the culture war is about a profound chasm in worldviews (e.g., Hunter, 1991). We first look at demographic variables (which fail to account for these cultural divides), then examine religion and religiosity among American elites.

THE ATTITUDINAL COMPONENTS OF BOURGEOIS RESTRAINT VERSUS EXPRESSIVE INDIVIDUALISM

In classical, Catholic, and traditional Calvinist thought, all human beings possess a common nature related to their humanity and their place in the cosmos, which ties them to, even as it separates them from, other species as part of a "great chain of being."

In the American case, Alexis de Tocqueville in *Democracy in America* (trans. 1969), Max Weber in *the Protestant Ethic and the Spirit of Capitalism* (trans. 1930), and more recently Louis Hartz in *The Liberal Tradition in America* (1955), among others, observed that America's uniqueness lay in its religious-cultural ethos. The Protestant ethic in the United States gave rise to both an economic-political freedom and a discipline of the passions. This tenuous balance between freedom and discipline enabled individuals to achieve their goals, on the basis of a strong, disciplined sense of self. The virtues consist of hard work, diligence, self-discipline, frugality, willpower, and rational foresight.

Contemporary American conservatism, however, blends aspects of our Puritan founding with nineteenth-century Victorianism, to create what historian Daniel Walker Howe (1977) calls the American Victorian synthesis. While many elements of this synthesis originated in the founding, it reached its highest degree of popular acclaim and acceptance from the period after the Civil War to the New Deal. These themes resonate in the thought of contemporary conservative intellectuals such as William F. Buckley, Jr., George Will, Michael Novak, and William Bennett. It is especially appropriate to consider modern conservatism as a direct descendent of the American Victorian synthesis, because whereas Puritans stated their beliefs in religious terms, the Victorians stated theirs in moral ones.

American Victorianism valued future-orientation and self-determination to a degree not found in the past. According to historian Gertrude Himmelfarb, American Victorians located responsibility and authority within the individual, promoting self-control, self-help, self-reliance, and self-discipline (1988, p. 231).

This did not mean that Victorians were in any way less certain of the truth of their beliefs than were the Puritans. "Victorians," notes Howe, "took their values seriously" (1977, p. 21). He says that Victorian thought was ultimately rooted in a belief in the objectivity and universality of moral principles. Victorians believed that morality and self-restraint substituted for law, just as law served as a substitute for force. Victorian culture, Howe points out, moved away from violence and toward persuasion as the primary mechanism for societal control (p. 20).

What we call expressive individualism is the liberal opposition to modern conservatism (or modern Victorianism). As discussed in chapter five, collectivistic liberalism was the major component of the American progressive-liberal tradition, but it was not the whole of the liberalism even during the first half of the twentieth century. Another theme is what Edward Shils (1980) calls the emancipationist tradition of contemporary liberalism and later calls the antinomian temptation (1988), what Daniel Bell (1978) calls modernism, or what Bellah and colleagues (1985) call expressive individualism.

According to Bellah et al. (1985), Emerson, Thoreau, and especially Whitman exemplified the notion of expressive individualism. Whitman explicitly rejected the moral codes of the prior era in favor of an truer expression of self and a release of the deeper human passions. Whitman's "Song of Myself" starts with the line "I celebrate myself and sing myself, And what I assume you shall assume" (quoted in Bartlett, 1965, p. 423)—a sentiment not widely held among American Victorians.[1]

In the 1920s, expressive individualism became the ideology of the American intellectual, serving as a debunking tool for disassembling the status quo. It received strong assistance from Sinclair Lewis's articulate attacks on the "mindless conformity" of Main Street and of George Babbitt, as well as from H. L. Mencken's pitiless ridiculing of the "booboisie" in his new, vastly popular journal, the American Mercury. Mencken's elitist scorn of the American public was exemplified in his famous wisecrack that no one ever went broke underestimating the intelligence of the American people.

This growing contempt for the popularly rooted Victorian culture dovetailed with the popularization of Freud and the increasing acceptance of expressionism in art, music, and literature (Coben, 1976) as well as the growing acceptance of child-centered expressiveness characteristic of much progressive education during the same period (Lerner, Nagai, and Rothman, 1995).

A few years later this contempt for traditional morality was exemplified by anthropologist Ruth Benedict's best-selling Patterns of Culture (1934), a text widely used in introductory anthropology classes. She states: "Tradition is as neurotic as any patient; an overgrown fear of deviation from its fortuitous standards conforms to all the usual definitions of the psychopathic. . . . It is probable that the social order of the

future will carry this tolerance and encouragement of individual difference further than any cultures of which we have experience" (p. 273).[2]

Part and parcel of the good life for the intellectual stratum thus
became the free expression of individual desires and pursuit of individual
passions. The core of this concept is the priority given to free, unfettered
expression of impulses, assumed to be good in and of themselves. It
rejects the traditional for the new and avant-garde. In short, the culture
of expressive individualism is centered around the exploration of experience and sensation—unfettered, impulsive, and nontraditional. An early
example of this impulse was given by Margaret Sanger, founder of
Planned Parenthood and the most important American advocate of birth
control. According to her most recent biographer, Sanger confided the
following to Progressive-era radical hostess Mabel Dodge: "[Sanger] told
us about the possibilities in the body for 'sex expression'; and as she sat
there, serene and quiet, and unfolded the mysteries and mightiness of
physical love, it seemed to us we had never known it before as a sacred
and at the same time a scientific reality" (Chesler, 1992, p. 96). Sanger
was the first person Dodge knew to be "openly an ardent propagandist
for the joys of the flesh" (ibid.).[3]

It follows that since the individual is the best judge of what is worth
pursuing for him or herself, no group has the right to decide collectively
what goals any other person should pursue. The purpose of government
becomes the protection of individual freedom from the larger polity, like
that described in J. S. Mill's classic work *On Liberty* (1947), where the
only legitimate restraint on liberty is to prevent direct physical harm to
others; for Mill, a person's own good is not sufficient warrant for state
coercion.

The 1960s brought many issues of expressive individualism into the
larger political debate. Previously, discussing human sexuality in public
had been taboo. In the case of abortion, as Kristen Luker in *Abortion and
the Politics of Motherhood* and others point out, pre-1960s abortion policy
consisted of a tacit bargain: laws that forbade abortion coexisted with
increasing numbers of abortions performed, officially to insure the
health of the mother but actually for diverse reasons. The intense politi-
cization of abortion began with the previously unheralded idea that
abortion is a woman's right, which subsequently made this kind of tacit
compromise impossible.

With the sexual revolution of the 1960s, the primacy of a right to
privacy, and the increasing receptivity for sex education in the public
schools, the ground was prepared for bringing issues of expressive individualism into the public arena. Traditional definitions of women's roles

became increasingly unpopular, no-fault divorce became widely accepted, and many laws against previously illegal sexual conduct were overturned by various court decisions, such as state laws forbidding the purchase of contraception (e.g., *Griswold* v. *Connecticut*). Luker, for example, reports that for many pro-choice activists, sex came to be seen as good in itself, primarily by providing pleasure and intimacy, growing "out of feelings experienced in the present rather than beliefs about what may happen in the future" (1984, p. 178).

The women's movement of the early 1970s also played a major role in bringing these issues of expressive individualism to the forefront of public debate. Social critic Barbara Ehrenreich, in a 1989 book review in the *New Republic*, recalls her first pregnancy: "I was angry . . . because in the process of giving birth something intrinsically womanly had been violated and insulted. It was this anger, this sense of violation and loss of control, that propelled me into feminism, and—by no means incidentally—into pro-choice activism" (p. 32). Pro-choice activism takes away any power or responsibility from men on the matter of abortion and puts it in the hands of women. In this sense, preserving the right to abortion is "as essential to the feminist movement as collective bargaining is to the trade union movement or racial equality to the civil rights movement," as Richard Polenberg succinctly phrased it in *Society* (1982).

The kinds of reasoning used by pro-choice activists to justify their positions reflect this view. Luker finds that pro-choice activists are believers in situation ethics—in part because they are moral pluralists (or, in Luker's account, moral relativists), regarding moral choices as often being between equally important values, and partly because they are also secularists and utilitarians, although not necessarily aware of these Benthamite roots. The right to choose has often been stated in precisely these terms: a woman, not society or her family, has a right to "control over her own body" and thus to decide whether to have an abortion. It is essentially a right to privacy, with sexual conduct a matter of choice among competing alternative lifestyles.

In somewhat different form, the right to privacy involves the issue of gay rights, also an outgrowth of the 1960s' sexual revolution and civil rights movement. Like the civil rights and feminist movements, the issue of discrimination is central, here based on a person's sexual orientation. In addition, the permitting of any sexual behavior between two consenting adults is, like the abortion issue, based on a fundamental right to privacy. While the Supreme Court (by a five-to-four vote) in *Bowers* v. *Hardwick* rejected the extension of this right to homosexuality and allowed sodomy laws to stand, it is by no means certain that this will continue to be the case. Whereas the feminist movement made significant political strides at the national level in the 1970s, the gay rights movement became a major player in presidential politics with the 1992 election of Bill Clinton. The furor over homosexuals in the military, Clinton's appointment of a record number of openly homosexual persons to office, and his executive order forbidding discrimination in federal employment on the basis of sexual orientation all point to the continuing centrality of this issue in the nation's culture wars.

The sexual revolution of the 1960s and the American feminist movement prepared the ground for publicly debating the merits of marriage, monogamy, virginity, abortion, and gay rights. The debate still goes on, but as our data show, few members of American elite groups support the conservative, American Victorian view.

Issues of Expressive Individualism

If Ruth Benedict were alive today, she would find that her prediction of a vastly more sexually tolerant society has been borne out, while Margaret Sanger would find a country in which school cheerleaders pregnant out of wedlock cannot be legally removed from their team. These policies largely reflect the success of American leaders in advancing their permissive views of expressive individualism. When we conducted our interviews in the late 1970s and early to mid-1980s, the gay rights movement was only beginning to emerge, yet a large majority of our elite respondents, as compared with the general public, supported not only the unconditional right to abortion but also the right of homosexuals to teach in public schools. Only 19 percent of the sample opposed a woman's right to choose abortion for whatever reason she wished. Only one-third (31 percent) of the sample believed that gays and lesbians should not teach in public schools, and less than a majority (47 percent) thought homosexual relations are wrong.

As one would expect, 75 percent of self-identified liberals strongly support abortion rights. However, 54 percent of self-labeled conservatives and 61 percent of moderates also support a woman's right to chose abortion. Even on the question of homosexuality, nearly 30 percent of conservatives, 48 percent of the moderates, and 69 percent of the liberals do not feel that homosexual relations are wrong. It should be stressed that these results predate the public emergence of the gay rights movement. If these questions were asked in the 1990s, it could be that a larger proportion of liberals and conservatives alike would find homosexuality acceptable. In another study, we found that philanthropy leaders, a relatively conservative group surveyed in 1989, exhibit a similar distribution of opinion on the subject among liberals and conservatives (Nagai, Lerner, and Rothman, 1994).

Surprisingly, adultery is the only form of sexual behavior that a large majority of American elites think wrong. Sixty-five percent of American leaders oppose a married person having sexual relations with someone who is not that person's spouse. Yet here, too, liberals are more relaxed about adultery than are conservatives. While 22 percent of conservatives do not condemn adultery, one-third of moderates, and 43 percent of the liberals are nonjudgmental in this area. Of those liberals who give themselves the maximum liberal score (a seven), only 45 percent condemn adultery.

Such widespread elite support represents at least a partial victory on the part of the adversary culture over traditional bourgeois attitudes. Differences on these issues are related to one's occupation, as shown in Table 6.1. In general, members of the cultural elites—such as the media, film, and television elites, as well as the public interest movement leaders—are the most liberal, while the traditional elites (business, military, religion) are the most conservative. For example, 59 percent of business leaders, 72 percent of religious elites, and 83 percent of the military elite think that homosexual relations are wrong.[4] At the other ideological extreme, 88 percent of public interest leaders, 72 percent of filmmakers, 76 percent of the media elite, and 77 percent of those in

TABLE 6.1   Agreement with Items Loading on Expressive Individualism Factor

	Right to Abortion	Homosexuality Is Wrong	Gays Should Not Teach	Adultery Is Wrong	N
Bureaucrats	81	48	34	67	200
Business	71	59	49	74	242
Congressional aides	81	54	30	68	134
Judges	80	66	38	66	114
Labor	87	61	40	73	95
Lawyers	90	40	19	62	150
Media	90	24	15	47	238
Military	73	83	70	82	152
Movies	97	28	13	42	96
Public interest	95	12	8	55	158
Religious leaders	38	72	37	89	178
Television	97	23	14	49	104
Total					1,861

Note: The exact wording of the questions is given in the appendix.

television disagree. In general the journalist, movie, public interest, and television elites score higher on the dimension of expressive individualism than all other groups; moreover, these differences are statistically significant.

DETERMINANTS OF EXPRESSIVE INDIVIDUALISM

Elites in the media, movies, television, and the public interest movement are significantly more liberal on issues of expressive individualism than are traditional elites. The values associated with support for expressive individualism, however, are not only associated with occupation, but intimately tied to religious belief and commitment.[5]

Table 6.2 shows the reestimated regression equation of several socio-demographic variables, parental socialization variables, religion, and expressive individualism.[6] Whatever may be true of the population as a whole, the region in which one was born and raised is unrelated to expressive individualism scores. In particular, Northerners are no more liberal on these issues than are Southerners. The only difference we find, after controlling for the other background variables, is between having been born in a foreign country and any of the other regions (or all of them averaged together). Respondents who are foreign born are more likely to support expressive individualism than are native-born elites (which is to be expected given the American Puritan-Victorian traditional view).

Statistically significant predictors include the respondents' sex and education. Women elites are more supportive of expressive individualism than are men, controlling for religion, region, mother's view, father's occupation, respondents' education, and occupation. In addition, the more educated respondents are, the more liberal they are on the expressive individualism factor, controlling for demographics. Lastly, religion is a significant predictor of elites' views on expressive individualism.

Religion and Political Ideology

We would expect elites who are religiously oriented to be less supportive of the views of sexuality proposed by proponents of expressive individualism than those who are unaffiliated, indifferent, or hostile to religion. Weber, Tocqueville, and Durkheim among others have noted the conflict between religiosity and expressive individualism. Weber writes of the inherent tension between religion and sex, but also argues that eroticism is at odds with rationality, self-control, and future planning. The rational regulation of marriage resolves the conflict:

Within this divine order it is given to man to live according to the rational purposes laid down by it and only according to them: to procreate and to rear children, and mutually to further one another in the state of grace. This inner-worldly rational asceticism must reject every sophistication of the sexual into eroticism as idolatry of the worst kind. In its turn, this asceticism gathers the primal, naturalist and unsublimated sexuality of the peasant into a rational order of man as creature. (Weber, 1946c, p. 349)

In a similar vein, Tocqueville in *Democracy in America* observed that religion in the United States, along with the family, was the institutional bulwark against the individualism and materialism otherwise characteristic of democratic societies (1969, pp. 442–49). Religion, he says, reminds us of our duties to each other and forces members of democracies away from an exclusive preoccupation with themselves as exemplified by extreme individualism, self-absorption, and materialism. While members of democratic societies are free to hold whatever opinions they choose, ultimately the proper balance between liberty and equality necessary for democratic society is based on morality, which in turn requires religion. Tocqueville, however, does not insist on a particular religion; he shows considerable indifference regarding explicit doctrines. In good sociological fashion, he focuses on religion's functionality.

How this process works in a more detailed fashion is suggested by the locus classicus of the functional view of religion, Emile Durkheim's *Elementary Forms of Religious Life* (1968). As Talcott Parsons points out, for Durkheim, the role of religious ritual, which is the point of church attendance, is to reinforce the attitudes of believers. In turn, the ritual itself brings these commonly shared attitudes into a great degree of self-consciousness, which strengthens individual commitment to them and thus strengthens the moral community (Durkheim, 1968; Parsons, 1968, p. 435).

Table 6.2 shows that Catholic elites are more likely to be conservative on issues of expressive individualism, while Jewish and nonreligious elites are more liberal on these matters compared with Protestants (all other things being equal). If our findings are correct, simply attending church should have a significant effect on expressive individualism. In addition, views of expressive individualism should predict respondents' views of the appropriate role of the church in society.

As Table 6.2 shows, there is a strong relationship between simple church attendance and belief in expressive individualism. Within each religious grouping, frequency of church attendance is negatively corre-

TABLE 6.2   Relative Influence of Mother's View and Frequency of Church Attendance on Expressive Individualism (standardized regression weights)

Mother's view	0.03
Church attendance	0.30*[1]
Religious affiliation	
Catholic	−0.14*
Protestant	−0.03
Jewish	0.03
Father's socioeconomic status	0.03
Occupation	
Bureaucrats	−0.12*
Business	−0.14*
Congressional aides	−0.14*
Judges	−0.14*
Labor	−0.10*
Lawyers	−0.04
Media	−0.02
Military	−0.24*
Movies	−0.01
Public interest	−0.04
Religious leaders	−0.22*
Race	0.02
Sex	0.12*
Education	0.06*
Town size	0.02
**Region	
South	0.00
Midwest	−0.03
West	−0.01
Foreign born	0.03
R-squared	0.38*
Change in R-squared (mother's view)	0.0012
Change in R-squared (church attendance)	0.0419

$N = 1,862.$ *Significant at $p \leq 0.05$.

**For each set of categorical predictors, such as occupation or region, one category is treated as the reference group. In this case, the regression weights represent the difference between each of the other regions and the Northeast.
[1] Church attendance coded 1 = every week, 4 = never.

lated with expressive individualism. If we include church attendance in the overall regression equation (presented earlier) predicting expressive individualism, we find that even controlling for parents' political views, father's occupational background, the specific religious tradition the respondent identifies with, education, sex, region of origin, and current occupation, the degree of church attendance strongly predicts expressive individualism (at the $p \leq 0.0001$ level of significance). In short, church attendance is far and away the strongest predictor of expressive individualism in the context of the full complement of demographic variables.

A second test considers respondents' views of how much influence religion should have. Those with higher scores on the expressive individualism scale should desire that the institution of religion have less influence and vice versa. The zero-order correlation between expressive individualism and the influence religion should have is -0.39, which is statistically significant at $p < 0.0001$. Including the standard series of controls, we find that expressive individualism remains a strong predictor of the influence religion should have at the $p \leq 0.0001$ level of significance, controlling for church attendance, religious affiliation, sex, and occupation (see Table 6.3).

We also examined the relationship between the amount of desired influence of feminist leaders and the degree of expressive individualism. If the reasoning on which our analysis is based is valid, subscribers to

TABLE 6.3   Relative Influence of Expressive Individualism on Preferred Influence of Religion

Expressive individualism	-0.11^*
Views on how much influence religion has**	0.23^*
Infrequency of church attendance	-0.27^*
Religious affiliation	
Catholic	0.08^*
Protestant	0.17^*
Jewish	-0.02^*
Occupation	
Bureaucrats	-0.02
Congressional aides	0.01
Judges	0.06^*
Labor	0.04
Lawyers	0.04
Military	0.03
Public interest	0.09^*
Sex	0.03
R-squared	0.34^*
Change in R-squared	0.0071

$N = 1,254$
*Significant at $p \leq 0.05$.
**Note: Respondents ranked on a seven-point scale how much influence they thought religion has, and how much influence religion should have, in American life today. The latter serves as the dependent variable.

expressive individualist doctrines should want to increase the influence of feminists, while those who dissent from expressive individualism are likely to seek to diminish feminist influence. The zero-order correlation between expressive individualism score and degree of desired feminist influence is 0.25, which is statistically significant at $p \leq 0.001$. When the analysis includes controls for gender, occupation, the influence feminists do have, and religious affiliation, expressive individualism remains a strong predictor of the desired degree of feminist influence ($p < 0.0001$) (see Table 6.4).

THE INFLUENCE OF SPECIFIC RELIGIOUS TRADITIONS. The presence of religious faith and commitment to religious institutions is a powerful pre-

TABLE 6.4   Relative Influence of Expressive Individualism on Preferred Influence of Feminism

Expressive individualism	0.22*
Influence feminists have**	0.31*
Infrequency of church attendance	0.03
Religious affiliation	
Catholic	−0.01
Protestant	−0.03
Jewish	−0.04
Occupation	
Bureaucrats	−0.08*
Business	−0.10*
Congressional aides	−0.08*
Judges	−0.01
Labor	0.04
Lawyers	−0.11*
Media	−0.07
Military	−0.11*
Movies	−0.04
Public interest	0.09*
Religious leaders	0.02
Sex	0.15*
R-squared	0.25*
Change in R-squared	0.031

$N = 1,691$
*Significant at $p < 0.05$.
**Note: Respondents ranked on a seven-point scale how much influence they thought feminists have, and how much influence feminists should have, in American life today. The latter serves as the dependent variable.

dictor of attitudes toward individualism. Brief examination of the specific doctrinal traditions of Protestantism, Catholicism, and Judaism suggests some religions are more hostile to expressive individualism than others. While a discussion of the specifics of these differing religious traditions is beyond the scope of this chapter and the expertise of its authors, some comment needs to be made. The Catholic position, tightly restricting sexuality with respect to birth control, abortion, and homosexuality, is well known, while Protestants have varied in the strictness of their prohibition. According to Ellen Chesler, Jews have never interpreted the famous discussion of onanism in Genesis to require as strict a prohibition as have Christians (Chesler, 1992, pp. 34–35).

Not surprisingly, religious affiliation has a strong independent effect on views toward expressive individualism. We collapsed elites' religious denominations into four categories: none, Catholic, Protestant, and Jewish.[7] Even controlling for social background and occupation, current religion has a significant impact on expressive individualism, but the largest gap is between Jewish and nonreligious elites versus Christians. The nonreligious have a mean expressive individualism score of 106.00, while Jewish elites have a mean score of 105.21, a difference that is not statistically significant.[8] Jewish elites are also more liberal than both Protestants (with a mean score of 97.54) and Catholics (93.37).[9]

THE JEWISH DIFFERENCE. Those of Jewish background, regardless of their current religious affiliation, are strikingly more liberal on issues of expressive individualism than are their gentile counterparts. Nonreligious Jews (i.e., those Jewish by ethnic identification only) are the most liberal ethnoreligious group of all, with a mean score of 107.69. Religious Jews, the second most liberal group, are as liberal as nonreligious Gentiles. Religious Jews have a mean score of 105.02, while nonreligious Gentiles score 105.40 on expressive individualism. Religious Gentiles are by far the most conservative group, with a mean score of 96.00. The differences between this group and all the other groups are statistically significant.

The major difference among Jewish elites is between the Orthodox Jews and the rest, although here too, Orthodox Jewish elites are significantly more liberal than are religious Gentiles, and far more liberal than the religious leaders of fundamentalist Protestantism. Orthodox Jewish elites have a mean score of 101.30 on expressive individualism; Conservatives average 104.49; Reform Jewish elites have a mean score of 105.64.[10]

Interestingly, religious affiliation also has an independent effect on the amount of influence respondents think the church should have. While it is not surprising that those with no religious affiliation desire religion to have less influence, it is notable that Jews and Catholics are both more likely to desire to reduce the influence of religion than are Protestants. Of course, the differences between Catholics and the more alienated groups—Jews and the nonreligious—are also statistically significant. Protestants wish religion to have the most influence, Catholics take an intermediate position, while Jews want religion to have the least influence. The only pairing that exhibits no statistically significant differences is between that of Jews and those with no religious affiliation. Clearly, Catholics, Jews, and the nonreligious identify the strength of organized religion with Protestantism and feel a corresponding sense of marginality with respect to it. Apparently, a vision of the once powerful Protestant establishment still exerts sway on the view of Catholics, Jews, and nonbelievers alike.

DISCUSSION

While there are clear and distinct Jewish differences and, to a lesser extent, a Protestant versus Catholic difference as well, traditional religious feeling and commitment act as the major brake against the values of expressive individualism.

As discussed earlier, religious ritual, as measured in our study by church attendance, reinforces the attitudes of the believers. Ritual makes believers more aware and more committed to their moral community. This explains the crucial role of church attendance in reinforcing traditional views toward expressive individualism. Traditional bourgeois (or Victorian) morality is shared to one degree or another by all the religious traditions.

The data show that contemporary Christian commitment is tied to a value that transcends individual rights, and certainly a right to privacy. Tocqueville declared, "Every religion places the object of man's desires outside and beyond worldly goods and naturally lifts the soul into regions far above the realm of the senses" (1969, p. 444). Those with an affinity to the traditional American Puritan-Victorian culture are mostly practicing Christians, where the focus is not on the immediacy of experience, and the religious impulse is transcendent and ascetic.

Daniel Bell states the contrast quite well. The culture of expressive individualism embodies what he calls the antinomian self, whereby the self becomes the source of moral judgment, and personal experience, not tradition or reason, becomes the source of understanding. It is in the very nature of religion, then, to impose a set of limits on the way in which any idea can be expressed in practice.

Because religious differences account for some of the differences in attitude toward expressive individualism, we believe the differences between "new class" groups and "traditional" groups may not be inherently one of occupation but rather of a new sensibility.[11] Ideas and the sentiments that underlie them do have consequences. At the same time, receptivity to these ideas is related to how one was raised, especially with regard to the political liberalism of one's mother.

SEVEN

COMPONENTS OF THE ADVERSARY CULTURE

Lionel Trilling coined the now commonplace phrase "adversary culture" to describe the thought and intention of modern intellectuals. The adversary culture judges and condemns the larger society, and seeks to replace values which undergird that society with its own. Yet while the concept quickly became part of the standard language for talking about the culture wars of contemporary society, it retains an elusive quality, making it difficult to connect up with standard empirical analyses of political ideology.

An important exception is the work of sociologist Paul Hollander. In his major work, *Anti-Americanism: Critiques at Home and Abroad, 1965–1990* (1992), he focuses on an important and neglected manifestation of the adversary culture—anti-Americanism. Hollander argues that this anti-Americanism is more than a collection of critiques of American society and American foreign policy. It is more than simple utopianism. It is, he claims, a mindset, "an attitude of distaste, aversion, or intense hostility the roots of which may be found in matters unrelated to the actual qualities or attributes of American society or the foreign policies of the United States" (p. viii). Hollander regards anti-Americanism as basically a hostile predisposition to anything American, much like a racist's hostility to anyone of another race, a sexist's hostility to one of the opposite sex, and the anti-Semite's hostility toward anything Jewish (ibid.).

Two further dimensions uncovered by our factor analysis are system alienation and regime threat, which reflect Hollander's notion of anti-

Americanism and allow us to obtain a more precise fix on the nature of the adversary culture. Membership in the adversary culture consists of those who score highly on a combination of these two independent dimensions.

SYSTEM LEGITIMACY VERSUS SYSTEM ALIENATION

Social theorists such as Bell, Kristol, and Gouldner take the view that the cultural "contradictions" of capitalism itself lead to the adversary culture: "Changes in cultural ideas have an imminence and autonomy because they develop from an internal logic at work within a cultural tradition. In this sense, new ideas and forms derive from a kind of dialogue with, or rebellion against, previous ideas and forms" (Bell, 1978, p. 54). The disjunction between the culture of the Puritan ethic and capitalism's own success has caused a decay of the traditional culture and an erosion of its legitimacy.

> Changes in culture as a whole, particularly the emergence of new life-styles, are made possible not only by changes in sensibility, but also by shifts in the social structure itself. One can see this most readily, in American society, in the development of new buying habits in a high consumption economy and the resultant erosion of the Protestant ethic and the Puritan temper, the two codes which sustained the traditional value system of American bourgeois society. (ibid., p. 55)

Affluence then is both the product and the death-knell of the culture of bourgeois capitalism. The economy of capitalism produces the affluence, the technology, the corporate structure, but also the consumption lifestyle that undercuts the very system of norms and values that gives capitalism its legitimacy. We are living off of the cultural capital of an earlier period, claims Irving Kristol (1978, p. 55). By this logic, the social order undercuts its own cultural justifications. Eventually, there is a crisis of legitimacy which focuses attention on this lack of fit between the cultural and social systems.

We propose a somewhat different view here. While the decay of the cultural systems of American Puritanism and the economic system of capitalism existed in a relationship of "non-fit" for many years, the kinds of changes that emerged were not inevitable. It was the series of events and happenings called "the sixties" that brought to the fore a systemwide crisis of legitimacy. The counterculture among the white-collar class popularized what we call system alienation, because the counterculture was precisely what it claimed to be—a culture in opposition to the prevailing orthodoxy. The 1960s, like other legitimation crises, was the event, the "happening" that disrupted the normal. While it may be true that contradictions of capitalism inevitably led to this crisis, it is more likely that without the 1960s intrusions, it might not have happened at all or at least not in the way it did.

The Sixties: System Crisis and the Alienated Aftermath

Sociologist Robert Nisbet notes, "An event is an intrusion" (1972, p. 26), and for many institutions, especially the universities and colleges, the 1960s were a massive intrusion. To be sure, one can find continuities and trends buried in the American past, yet social thinkers of the prior decade were proclaiming the end of ideology, only to be faced with the eruption of social movements, violent confrontations, and proclamations for the end of American society as we knew it.

The student movements of the sixties have been subject to much commentary and research, often portrayed in the most flattering sense of possessing a higher order of morality and consciousness. Speaking of these students as the vanguard of the postindustrial society, Kenneth Keniston describes their anti-bourgeois orientations with enthusiasm: "To [the radical young], the psychological imperatives, social institutions and cultural values of the industrial ethic seem largely outdated and irrelevant to their own lives" (1971, p. 311). He argues that, substituting for the bourgeois culture, "the new revolution also involves a continuing struggle against psychological or institutional closure or rigidity in any form, even the rigidity of a definite adult role. Positively, it extols the virtues of openness, motion, and continuing human development" (p. 314).

Intellectuals of the New Left wrote for the New York Times, their books became best-sellers, and many ended up as part of the very institutions under attack. The universities and industries of mass culture were powerfully influenced by the New Left. In earlier decades, intellectuals were outside academic institutions, but from the 1960s onward, as a result of the massive expansions of the university and college system, most garden-variety intellectuals came to reside within the academy. The expansion of the alienated culture occurred within an institutionalized setting that enabled its rapid diffusion to the larger upper-middle-class white-collar professional public. As a result, the sixties and postsixties college students questioned not merely the efficacy of institutions, but also their underlying legitimacy.[1]

The Efficacy Versus Legitimacy of Power

Political authority can be supported on the basis of its efficacy, that is, how well government does what it promised to do. If the government is to improve race relations, but riots increase in number, then the government is obviously not efficacious. Authority in this case is not living up to its responsibilities.

Fundamentally, however, we obey political authority because of its legitimacy. We accept the justification of political authority on the basis of the claim that its power to act the way it does is morally right. To challenge its moral rightness is to call into question the legitimacy of the political order.[2]

When an institution's legitimacy is challenged, that institution cannot engender compliance, either because its actions are deemed to lie outside the domain of what is defined to be proper, or because the whole basis of authority itself is thought to be unjust. By this analysis then, one can reject the command of the president on the basis of the claim that his command lies outside what is properly defined as the president's legal sphere of action. But one can also reject the command of the president on the basis of nonrecognition of the presidency as an office to which one ought to swear allegiance.

The New Left critique was not centered around questions of government efficacy, nor was it centered around whether government exceeded its scope of authority. The New Left rejected the legitimacy of political authority. It declared null and void the traditional political values that ultimately granted to political authority the rightness to act.

In the view of the New Left, the social order of bourgeois-liberal society is inherently dehumanizing and repressive. For the New Left, the self seeks to be free as authority seeks to oppress; self and authority are in inherent conflict. The affluent society and its technology cannot provide the sum and substance for a good society; the culture of mass society caters to trivial and vulgar satisfactions; the sciences, technology, and the professions perpetuate conditions of inequality; and the trapping of liberal democracy such as individual rights and majority rule all mask the true nature of oppressive power.

The New Left embodied the seemingly disjointed convergence of extreme sexual libertarianism, advocacy of drug use, a rejection of science and technology, and a rejection of the professional standards and ethics of such professions as academia, journalism, law, and medicine, and a promotion of membership in communes—all expressed in a revolutionary, nihilistic rhetoric.

Moreover, much of the language and meanings of the New Left were radically foreign to the 1930s revolutionaries and fellow travelers, despite the fact that many of the activities and social movements bear a marked resemblance. While the political radicalism of the 1930s viewed socialism or Communism as the natural culmination of science, progress, and reason, the rhetoric of the 1960s rejected it. Rather than exist apart from the major institutions as did the intellectuals of the 1920s, the proponents of the eruptive language of the 1960s sought to form a new culture and social order as a vehicle for true self-emancipation.

What were the effects of the New Left's attack on the legitimacy of the American system? We believe that despite its collapse as an organized group, the New Left had far-reaching effects on American society. One such effect is the active presence of system alienation versus system legitimacy as an independent dimension of contemporary American ideology, not merely as a fringe phenomenon, but as existing in some considerable quantity at the heart of American institutions. The musings of Hillary Rodham Clinton on the necessity for a "politics of meaning" (Kelly, 1993) a phrase used by veteran sixties activist and editor of *Tikkun* magazine Michael Lerner (no relation to the first co-author) and quondam advisor to the first lady, demonstrate exactly how powerful the influence of the sixties still is.

Hollander (1992) defines the adversary culture in its current form as a pervasive, intense, and general resentment of American society. He links the roots of alienation from the system to the idea of "repressive tolerance" (p. 60). Alienated intellectuals assume that the United States oppresses countries abroad (i.e., less developed nations). Oppression at home, however, is more subtle; only leftist intellectuals have the insight and critical facility to discern it. Others suffer from false consciousness, even though they think they are free. In the eyes of the intellectual left, American life is one of "insensitivity, brutality, propensity to violence, and aggressive competitiveness peculiar to Americans" (Hollander, 1992, p. 62).

In addition to Hollander, sociologists Edward Shils (1980) and Daniel Bell (1978) emphasize the pervasiveness of this sense of alienation from America within the colleges and universities. The alienation of the professoriat (especially in the humanities and social sciences) pervades all levels, from the elite Ivy League schools to the branch campuses of the smallest city college. Even leftist philosopher Richard Rorty concedes that the problem with this left is that it is "unpatriotic," refuses "to rejoice in the country it inhabits . . . [and] repudiates the idea of a national identity" and "the emotion of national pride" (Rorty, 1994, p. E-15).

In the larger popular culture, film critic Michael Medved similarly notes the pervasiveness of anti-Americanism. Popular films are anti-military, antipolice, and antibusiness. Many movies, claims Medved, por-tray American society as "cruel, corrupt, and hopelessly unjust" (1992, p. 223). It is thus no accident that the sixties receive the most attention from Hollywood, and that filmmakers use the Vietnam War for a general condemnation of America; it is, says Medved, "Hollywood's favorite war" (p. 227).[3]

Our data analysis shows that six questions form this underlying dimension which we call system legitimacy versus system alienation. The questions are: Does the American legal system mainly favor the wealthy? Is the American private enterprise system generally fair to working people? Does the United States need a complete restructuring of its basic institutions? Should big corporations be taken out of private ownership and run in the public interest? Does the structure of our society cause most people to feel alienated? And lastly, has the main goal of U.S. foreign policy been to protect American business interests? (Al-though it was not available for all groups, and thus is not used here, our subsequent factor analysis found that the question on whether the United States should move toward socialism loaded heavily on this factor.)

These issues measure a general predisposition toward the United States as a whole. They link views on the legitimacy of the judicial system, the economic system, private ownership, and American national interests abroad, as well as views on American social structure. They are independent of the free market versus collectivist liberalism dimension discussed in chapter five. One could be in favor of increasing the policies associated with collectivistic liberalism, such as guaranteed universal employment and heavy taxation of the rich, while still believing in the American system as a whole. Many New Dealers clearly held such be-liefs.[4] Most members of new strategic elites think less of the efficacy and legitimacy of the American political system than do traditional elites. Certain groups are in fact extremely hostile to the American system as a whole.

ELITE SUPPORT OR ALIENATION FROM THE SYSTEM

Most members of the strategic elites we studied generally support the system (see Table 7.1). Analysis of individual questions, however, yields some surprising results. Seventy-three percent of American elites think that the legal system favors the wealthy. If we examine the data by

TABLE 7.1 Elite Opinion on System Legitimacy Questions (percentage agree)

	Legal System Favors Wealthy	Foreign Policy Supports Business	Big Corporations Should Be Publicly Owned	Private Enterprise Is Fair to Workers	Social Structure Causes Alienation	System Needs Overhaul
Bureaucrats	76	43	4	82	27	21
Business	65	31	6	90	29	31
Congressional aides	71	40	18	69	37	25
Judges	40	30	6	78	31	19
Labor	81	67	22	42	45	49
Lawyers	54	29	1	84	23	9
Media	88	50	13	70	49	27
Military	68	25	3	94	10	20
Movies	88	75	16	67	63	52
Public interest	92	74	38	30	75	48
Religious leaders	77	55	19	64	40	42
Television	76	73	21	69	58	46
Total average sample	73	47	13	71	39	31

occupation, we find that even business executives and military leaders, generally the most conservative of groups, believe this to be the case. The two groups that are part of the legal establishment (federal judges and corporate lawyers) are the only ones in which large majorities do not think the legal system favors the rich. Forty percent of judges think the legal system favors of the rich, and a bare majority of corporate lawyers agree. As expected, almost all public interest leaders, a group that includes many lawyers, think the legal system is biased in favor of the well-to-do.

In contrast, elites are sharply divided on the question as to whether American foreign policy is designed to favor the interests of big business. Forty-seven percent of all elites think that the protection of big business is the primary goal of American foreign policy. This includes roughly three-fourths of the movie elite, public interest leaders, and the television elite, and two-thirds of labor leaders. Other elites disagree. An overwhelming proportion of business leaders, the judiciary, lawyers, and the military elite do not agree with the proposition.

Despite the antipathy toward big business felt by many elites, only minorities of even the most liberal elite groups favor public ownership of big corporations. Thirty-eight percent of the public interest leaders favor such nationalization, while only 22 percent of the labor leaders and 21 percent of television writers, producers, and directors agree. (In response to another question asked of only a few groups, however, 51 percent of the public interest elite favor moving toward socialism.)

Most members of our elite sample (71 percent) also think the American economic system of private enterprise is generally fair to workers. Only those elites with the largest stake in opposing American business—labor and public interest leaders—dissent from that proposition. Only 42 percent of labor and 30 percent of public interest leaders believe that private enterprise is fair to workers, in contrast with a majority of those in every other elite group.

Most respondents appear satisfied with the way things are. Most do not think that the American system necessarily produces alienation, although large majorities of the movie and television elite and the public interest leaders disagree. Moreover, 31 percent of American elites think U.S. institutions need to be overhauled. Nearly a majority of labor and public interest elites, who are among the most dissatisfied, agree, along with a majority of filmmakers and a near majority of television writers, producers, and directors. The media elite, however, are more content; only 27 percent think American institutions need to be overhauled—roughly the same proportion as the business elite.

Table 3.3 lists average alienation scores for each group. Individual scores range from a low of 78.16, the most supportive of the system, to a high of 128.81, the most alienated. There are large differences between elite groups. Corporate lawyers and public interest leaders are nearly 1.5 standard deviations apart. Aside from lawyers and the business elite, the least alienated groups are in the government: judges, the military, and federal civil servants. In contrast, elite groups on the outside—public interest leaders, labor, and cultural elites—are much more alienated from the system.

A more extensive regression analysis of the sources of alienation, including various controls, shows that public interest leaders are still the most alienated from the system (see Table 5.3). The only change is the relative decline of labor leaders from third most alienated to fifth most alienated. Members of traditional elite occupations—the bureaucracy, business leaders, congressional aides, judges, lawyers, and military leaders—are significantly attached to the United States, all other things being equal, while cultural elites, especially television makers, movie writers, producers, and directors, religious leaders, and the public interest group leaders, remain the most alienated of groups.

Various background measures are significantly related to attitudes of alienation.[5] Father's liberalism, but not father's class status, is positively related to system alienation.[6] In addition, blacks and women, all other things being equal, are more alienated than are whites and males. So are Jewish and nonreligious elites relative to Protestants and Catholics. While attaining elite status may be more meritocratic than ever before, elite blacks, women, Jews, and the nonreligious feel marginal to the American system. The notion of American society as unfairly biased toward white Christian males continues to resonate with these elites.

We have shown how system alienation makes up the third component of American liberalism. In terms of social background, the new class occupations (or being Jewish, female, or black) are significantly related to feelings of alienation. Being alienated is only one portion of the adversary culture. Its second aspect is that it sees no enemies on the left, either at home or abroad.

No Enemies on the Left: Debating Communism and Crime

While treating the two issue areas of Communism and crime as a unity may appear strange, some reflection shows that positions taken in these areas reveal an underlying core value. The core value centers around separating "us," that is, the in-group from "them," outsiders, the out-groups.

Sociologist William Graham Sumner invented the terms *in-group* versus *out-group* and emphasized the social fact that every group divides the world into itself and everyone else, preferring us to them.[7] Social scientists now treat this distinction as a fundamental fact of social life, and Sumner's concepts have become a standard part of any introductory sociology text.

This underlying dimension that combines anti-Communists and criminals corresponds with analytical types of political culture presented by the late Aaron Wildavsky (1991) and also with the values measures proposed by Ronald Inglehart (1977). Our ideological dimensions overlap with Wildavsky's typology of political cultures, and aspects of his egalitarian culture correspond to our regime threat view. Radical egalitarians are likely to take a more relaxed view of foreign adversaries and crime than are adherents to the other political cultures. It is not that they necessarily regard the threats as less significant; rather, given their hostility to the system, such threats do not concern them. Indeed, as immortalized in Jean-Paul Sartre's admiration for the writer-criminal Jean Genet, they may even (consciously or unconsciously) welcome attacks on the "oppressive" bourgeois moral order (Hayman, 1987).

Wildavsky's hierarchical culture (and on other issues, his individualist culture) corresponds with our conservative position on regime threat. The hierarchicalist is concerned with foreign enemies; he or she seeks to restrict civil rights and is sympathetic to certain forms of censorship. Wildavsky's enumeration of ideological types is an a priori construction. It is not based on the analysis of any body of empirical data. Our survey suggests that the issues with which he is concerned are best described along rather different dimensions than he outlines.

Inglehart's theory of postmaterialism (1977) is based on Abraham Maslow's theory of personality (1970). Inglehart argues that human beings respond to a hierarchy of needs, proceeding from material to aesthetic and intellectual needs. As the former are satisfied, persons become interested in the latter. Inglehart contends that changes in modern society have produced a new, postmaterialist constellation of values, which he contrasts with previously dominant materialist (or bourgeois) values. His twelve value choices include six categories of materialist values. Within the materialist values are two types, material needs and safety needs. Our outsider threat dimension is similar to Inglehart's safety needs, a category that includes "maintaining order," "fighting crime," and "making sure the country has strong defense forces" (pp. 40–41).[8]

If we examine the debate between conservatives and liberals on issues of foreign threat and crime, we find a similarity of language when
debating these two seemingly disparate topics. Those who feel that a
significant degree of external threat exists in foreign relations are conservatives, or "hawks," while those who disagree are liberals, or "doves."
Until the fall of Communism, conservatives were suspicious of the Soviet
Union and supportive of a strong military, increased defense spending,
anti-Communist regimes, and anti-Communist insurgences. The underlying conservative view was that the Soviet Union posed a mortal threat
to the safety and survival of the United States.

Radical critics, however, linked together "aggression abroad and repression at home, American imperialism and domestic social injustice"
(Hollander, 1992, p. 69). After the Vietnam War, many radicals and even
liberals came to regard Communism as a minimal or even nonexistent
threat to the American regime. They viewed the conflict between the
United States and the Soviet Union as basically manageable by arms
control agreements. The more significant issues of foreign affairs concerned North-South relations, particularly human rights violations
among right-wing authoritarian countries allied to the United States, for
example, El Salvador and South Korea. William Sloan Coffin observes:
"We see the effects of the arms race everywhere—rotting, rat-infested
housing, inadequate programs of health care and education, rampant
unemployment . . . the poor . . . have become modern-day lepers in this
country while we spend billions upon billions on armaments" (quoted in
ibid., p. 70).

There is a similar conceptual split in the arena of law and order.
Conservatives feel that rising crime rates pose a great threat to social
order. This core value manifests in support for capital punishment, long
prison sentences for criminals, and a minimum of procedural rights for
defendants. Liberals believe that crime is a product of societal injustice,
to be dealt with by education and rehabilitation and changing the system
which produces crime; consequently, they oppose the measures conservatives support. During the 1960s, as Scammon and Wattenberg (1970)
point out, law and order, the conservative slogan, was juxtaposed against
peace and justice, the liberal slogan. In addition, liberals favor increasing
intervention by the courts in many matters (judicial activism), while
conservatives believe in the contrary position, usually identified as judicial restraint.

In short, conservatives, whether they are talking about crime or
foreign policy, employ similar arguments and even language; the same is
true for liberals. Questions of deterrence play a major role in discussion

of the court system's leniency and the use of capital punishment. They also play a role in views on the Soviet Union (and, more recently, Iraq), the necessity of having a strong military force, and subsidizing a defense buildup, often with high-tech weapons, to contain Soviet power. It is equally reasonable to speak of deterring criminals and hostile foreign powers.

The problem of ascertaining the just use of force is also common to both subject areas. Self-defense is normally considered justified. The debate between conservatives and liberals concerns the definition of whether certain actions qualify as self-defense or are unnecessarily provocative. In the foreign policy arena, the issue is often put in terms of arms control and nuclear proliferation. Regarding criminal justice, questions revolve around the utility of gun control.

A third commonality concerns law and the behavior of outsiders. A common liberal argument is that crime is the product of social circumstances, society, or "us." This argument is often phrased in terms of crime's "root causes" (such as poverty). Liberals discount the criminal's individual responsibility and argue for the rehabilitative, lenient treatment of criminals and changing the system that produces criminals. In contrast, conservatives tend to stress individual responsibility and punishment.

Soviet leaders took an extreme position on this subject. Before coming to power and even in the early days of power, they saw criminality as a function of the bourgeois system and stressed rehabilitation, except for supporters of the old regime, whom they dealt with punitively. Later, however, the regime became increasingly conservative on questions of criminality, even to the point of restoring and emphasizing the notion of personal responsibility (Rothman, 1970, pp. 635–62).

Similarly, in the foreign policy field, liberals argue that the "outside" power is really acting either for reasons of self-defense to prevent encirclement (in response to our perceived aggression) or in response to just grievances accumulated by our past treatment of them. Hollander (1982, 1992) quotes extensively from many American critics, the political pilgrims, who downplayed human rights abuses by China, Vietnam, and Cuba, among others, in their pilgrimage to find an anti-American salvation abroad. Anti-American critics made a recent pilgrimage to Sandinista-controlled Nicaragua:

> The attractions of Nicaragua under the Sandinistas were no different from the appeals of other state socialist systems of the past. As its American supporters saw it, Nicaragua was attempting to establish an egalitarian society, implement social justice, uplift the poor, over-

come backwardness, create a moral community, encourage genuine political participation, and restore the increasingly discredited doctrines of socialism. As such it was, in the eyes of these beholders, diametrically opposed to everything they rejected in their own society; its alleged victimization by the United States helped to prove and reaffirm their beliefs in the incorrigible flaws of American society and culture. Support of Nicaragua thus became an essential part of the critique of the United States. (ibid., p. 291)

Hollander's formulation joins together anti-American system alienation with a disbelief in regime threat. Our data analysis, however, shows that they are two separate dimensions of liberalism, although many individuals, especially among academics and intellectuals, hold both views simultaneously. This conjoining creates confusion for those who are not alienated from America, but who sincerely (perhaps naively) think other regimes do not threaten the United States. The noninterventionist views of former Secretary of State Cyrus Vance, for example, reflect the no-regime-threat position of people who are clearly not alienated from the American system.

EMPIRICAL RESULTS

The appropriate test of our argument, relating concepts to indicators, is factor analysis. This allows the extraction of underlying dimension(s) from bivariate correlations among individual attitudes. We have previously used this technique because of our belief in the multidimensionality of contemporary political ideology. Our initial data analysis was based on seventeen questions asked of all twelve elite groups, resulting in three dimensions: laissez-faire versus collectivist liberalism, Puritan restraint versus expressive individualism, and system support versus system alienation. The next dimension, regime threat versus no regime threat, emerged from a factor analysis of thirty questions asked only of the eight elite groups surveyed in the mid-1980s (bureaucrats, congressional aides, judges, labor leaders, lawyers, the military, public interest leaders, and the religious elite). The dimension of regime threat versus no regime threat contains four items consisting of a combination of defense issues and questions of criminal justice (Table 3.1). While these are usually seen as separate arenas of public debate, our data analysis shows that positions taken on either issue are not only related, but actually reflective of positions on a single underlying dimension.[9]

This analysis produces four dimensions—system alienation, collectivist liberalism, expressive individualism, and our main concern here, the dimension that combines some foreign policy issues and views about crime.

Analysis of these individual items shows that many elites in the 1980s did not favor a strong, hawkish position on foreign policy. Even though the Reagan administration portrayed the USSR as the evil empire, only the military elite consistently favored the vigorous use of force against America's enemies (see Table 7.2).

Eighty percent of the military believed we should be more forceful with the USSR, even at the risk of war. Less than half the labor leaders and congressional aides took the same position, while even smaller percentages of other groups agreed. Only 9 percent of public interest leaders believed that a more forceful stand against the Soviet Union was called for. Similarly, 60 percent of the military favored having the strongest defense in the world, but most other elites disagreed; again the public interest group elite was the least supportive, with only 3 percent agreeing. Despite elites' overwhelming aversion to using military force, however, most elite members were willing to let the CIA engage in covert action to overthrow hostile governments. Most federal bureaucrats, congressional aides, labor leaders, lawyers, and the military supported such methods by the CIA. Only 26 percent of public interest group leaders agreed.

Not surprisingly, 90 percent of the military and 61 percent of trade union leaders thought the courts are too supportive of criminal rights.[10] Only 13 percent of public interest group leaders felt likewise.

The occupational differences on the regime threat factor are summarized in Table 3.3. Briefly, the public interest elites differ from the military by nearly two standard deviations and are significantly more liberal on this dimension than all other groups except judges and religious leaders.

Viewing the results of a regression analysis, we find that members of certain elite groups are inclined to perceive threats—the military, bureaucrats, and congressional aides. Labor leaders (controlling for demographic variables) also favor the use of force against enemies, despite their high sense of alienation from the system and their high degree of self-identified liberalism (see Table 5.3).

Few social background variables are related to this regime threat dimension. All other things being equal, the better educated are less likely to see threats against the regime than are persons with less formal education. Those whose fathers are liberal react in the same manner.

TABLE 7.2 Views Constituting the Regime Threat Dimension (percentage agree)

	Bureaucrats	Congressional Aides	Judges	Labor	Lawyers	Military	Public Interest	Religious Leaders
We should be forceful toward USSR	33	43	30	43	34	80	9	32
U.S. military should be strongest	25	37	31	34	34	60	3	27
CIA overthrows are sometimes necessary	60	63	48	55	62	86	26	36
Too much concern for criminals	73	66	29	61	39	90	13	51

Note: Exact wording of questions is given in the appendix.

Race and gender have no effect. Religion as measured by religious affiliation (and by frequency of church attendance) has no relationship to beliefs about regime enemies.

The Persistence of Crime as Part of the Regime Threat Dimension

To test the unidimensionality of the regime threat scale, we factor analyzed these four items alone, as suggested by Marradi (1981). This method is a useful test of the stability of the dimension. Only one factor could be extracted. The loadings of these four items are comparable to the previous results.[11]

To test further the argument that national defense and crime questions comprise a single dimension, a second factor analysis was performed, using all the survey questions plus others from a sample of the philanthropic elite (Nagai, Lerner, and Rothman, 1994). Here, too, we found the same dimensions as in the elite samples. In the analysis of the philanthropic elite, responses to a question about capital punishment were added, which provided a greater possibility that the crime questions would emerge as statistically separate from the foreign policy questions. Nonetheless, we obtained results similar to our previous analysis. The two crime questions and three foreign policy questions regarding foreign threats load on the rotated factor. This factor analytic result was also subject to yet another factor analysis (as suggested by Marradi, 1981), wherein the five questions asked of the philanthropic elite were factored to see if they formed a single dimension. They did so, confirming the earlier results.[12]

Other studies have found similar correlates between issues of crime and defense. The Center for Political Studies' 1988 National Election Study contains data that allow for a modest extension.[13] Mass opinion is far less structured by a consistent ideology compared with opinion among elites. As a result, any correlation is likely to be weaker than any among elites (e.g., Converse, 1964; Lerner, Nagai, and Rothman, 1991). There is nevertheless a statistically significant (though small) correlation in the appropriate direction ($r = -0.12$, $p < 0.01$) between a question asking for respondents' opinion on capital punishment and a question asking for their views on the Soviet Union. This is further external support for the existence of the underlying regime threat dimension.

Sociologist Allen Barton's study of American elites finds a similar correlation between foreign policy regarding the Soviet Union and crime (e.g., Barton, 1975; W. Parsons, 1976; Barton and Parsons, 1977). Barton and his colleagues found a high correlation ($r = 0.61$) between what he labels a foreign policy scale and what he calls a civil liberties scale; the latter contains two questions on law and order issues, suggestive of a common underlying factor, which his co-author and student Wayne Parsons recognizes but fails to elaborate on (see Parsons, 1976, pp. 37–47).

In sum, we find a hitherto unexpected commonality between issues of law and order and issues of foreign policy toughness. The existence of this regime threat dimension exhibits considerable stability and consequently is a worthy object of continued investigation. We have no doubt that differences in views on the use of force abroad will still structure the thought of Americans, in close association with their views on law and order; both issues remain salient to many.

THE IMPACT OF IDEOLOGY: USING FORCE AND VIEWING THE WORLD

As discussed in chapter four, ideology structures our views of the world when the old culture will do no longer. Alienation from the system and opposition to the use of force against one's enemies, more than the other dimensions of liberalism, form the coherent alternative worldview that many critics call the adversary culture.

These dimensions are statistically related to perceptions of institutional power more systematically than are the other dimensions. As a person becomes more alienated from the system, he or she attributes more power to business and military leaders; a person increasingly opposed to the use of force also assigns increasing power to the military.

Considering attitudes toward intellectuals also supports our contention that alienation and opposition to the use of force constitute the adversary culture. The intellectual is central to this modern anti-Americanism. The more alienated and pacifist a person is, the more she or he thinks intellectuals have little power. Collectivist liberalism, however, is positively related to perceptions about the power intellectuals have and should have: the higher a person's collectivist liberalism score, the more power he or she attributes to intellectuals. (The data are presented in chapter four.)

Statistical analysis of these ideological dimensions and of Inglehart's materialist versus postmaterialist goals also supports our notion of the adversary culture being composed of these two ideological strands. A logistic regression analysis shows that only these two dimensions, system alienation and no regime threat, are significantly related to selecting one of Inglehart's postmaterialist goals.

When it comes to evaluating the reliability of intellectual journals, the more alienated people are, the more they attribute significantly greater reliability to the *New York Review of Books* and the *Nation,* but the more likely they are to consider *Commentary* unreliable. Reluctance to use force against enemies, however, is significantly but inversely related to only two intellectual journals, the *National Review* and *Commentary,* both noteworthy for their anti-Communism.

The relationship between these ideological dimensions and approval ratings of prominent individuals also supports our contention that together they make up a distinctive culture that is antagonistic toward American institutions. On a scale of one (strongly disapprove) to seven (strongly approve), respondents were asked to rate several prominent figures or groups: Ronald Reagan, Margaret Thatcher, Fidel Castro, the Sandinistas, the Moral Majority, Ted Kennedy, Ralph Nader, Jeanne Kirkpatrick, John Kenneth Galbraith, Milton Friedman, Andrew Young, and Gloria Steinem. The four ideological dimensions taken together do a good job of accounting for the approval ratings of these political figures (see Table 7.3). If we examine standardized regression coefficients for Fidel Castro, the Sandinistas, and Andrew Young, however, system alienation and opposition to the use of force against enemies have much more predictive power than do the other dimensions.[14]

In short, the ideological dimensions of alienation and regime threat significantly affect perceptions of the outside world: institutional power, media reliability, larger societal goals, and major media figures. As a group, all these components show the persistence of the adversary culture. It seems clear that, for these individuals, the juxtaposition of hostility to the use of force against ideological enemies and criminals is of a piece and does not necessarily reflect a pacifist outlook. After all, by the mid-1980s it was clear that the Castro regime was quite willing to rely on force and was not particularly concerned with the human rights of its citizens. For some Americans, then, it is not opposition to force per se that determines their positions. Rather, they do not wish to use force against those whom they see as critics (implicit or explicit) of American bourgeois society.

Our data show, moreover, that all liberals do not necessarily partake of this culture. Many who define their liberalism primarily as expressive individualism or collectivist liberalism, or both, are not part of the anti-American radical critique. The expressive individualists-collectivist lib-

TABLE 7.3   Ideological Dimensions of Liberalism and Rating Political
Figures: Regression Analysis

	Ted Kennedy	Jeanne Kirkpatrick	John K. Galbraith
System alienation	0.2903*	−0.2864*	0.2090*
Collectivist liberalism	0.3137*	−0.2253*	0.2632*
Expressive individualism	0.1826*	−0.1353*	0.1594*
Regime threat	0.1579*	−0.2314*	0.1535*
N	1,044	1,013	1,010
	Ronald Reagan	Fidel Castro	Sandinistas
System alienation	−0.3096*	0.3121*	0.3296*
Collectivist liberalism	−0.3920*	−0.0071	0.1218*
Expressive individualism	−0.2732*	0.1600*	0.0922*
Regime threat	−0.2345*	0.2564*	0.2581*
N	1,040	1,037	967
	Margaret Thatcher	Milton Friedman	Andrew Young
System alienation	−0.3666*	−0.3083*	0.2681*
Collectivist liberalism	−0.2867*	−0.2960*	0.1020*
Expressive individualism	−0.1343*	−0.1305*	0.1038*
Regime threat	−0.2151*	−0.1485*	0.3180*
N	1,039	962	1,029
	Moral Majority	Ralph Nader	Gloria Steinem
System alienation	−0.1197*	0.2263*	0.2108*
Collectivist liberalism	−0.2052*	0.2930*	0.1520*
Expressive individualism	−0.3618*	0.1548*	0.3887*
Regime threat	−0.1682*	0.1095*	0.1542*
N	1,043	1,044	990

*$p \leq 0.05$ level of significance or better.

erals do not look at institutional power, societal goals, and intellectual journals with such systematic antagonism. Similarly, one could be a pacifist or a socialist and not partake of the adversary culture. Proponents of the adversary culture do not merely disagree with conservatives and other liberals on specific policy issues; among America's radical critics, the hostility runs deep.

EIGHT

PERSONALITY, FAMILY, AND IDEOLOGY

Until this point, we have focused on social background factors such as religious affiliation, ethnicity, gender, and father's ideology as key variables in explaining ideological differences among elites. In this chapter, we examine the relationship between personality and ideology. We also examine the relationship between membership in a particular elite group and ideology.

In *Roots of Radicalism* Rothman and Lichter (1982, pp. 49–79) discuss extensively the political biases and methodological flaws in the most prominent studies of personality and ideology from the 1950s and 1960s. They note that there are "virtually hundreds of studies that seem to prove that radical students were democratic rather than authoritarian, humanitarian and humanistic rather than pragmatic and self-interested, and generally psychologically healthy and morally advanced" (p. 52).[1]

Many of these studies, they argue, arrive at this conclusion because it is built into their assumptions. Questions purporting to measure personality traits are really measuring ideology and defining positive personality traits by their ideological stance. While this may seem self-evident, Rothman and Lichter (1982, pp. 53–72) demonstrate the myriad ways in which what are claimed to be positive personality attributes are actually liberal values. One set of examples can be derived from a prominent personality inventory, the Omnibus Personality Inventory (OPI). As Rothman and Lichter point out, OPI items comprising personal autonomy include issue attitudes that really measure one or another dimension of political liberalism. For example, the statements "It is not the duty of a citizen to support his country right or wrong" and "Disobedience to the government is sometimes justified" measure personal autonomy on the OPI, but also reflect system alienation. Another positive indicator of personal autonomy, "Divorce is often justified," measures expressive individualism.

The OPI also includes a "nonauthoritarianism" scale, which Rothman and Lichter observe is merely a modification of the notorious F (fascism) scale. These scales, which purport to measure authoritarian versus nonauthoritarian traits, in fact measure conservatism versus liberalism (see Rothman and Lichter, 1982, for summary, pp. 59–61).

Nor is the only problem operational independence of personality and ideology measures. Even the best nonbiased cognitive multiple choice or sentence completion tests of personality are flawed, especially when administered to sophisticated respondents. Such tests generally provide only a picture of the respondent's public self-image, not because respondents prevaricate but rather because relatively few people are capable of genuine self-reflection. The more sophisticated the respondent, the more complex his or her defenses. On most written tests, sophisticated respondents often present an image of their ideal rather than real self.[2] For this reason, Rothman and Lichter relied on the Thematic Apperception Test (TAT) and its methodology to study the radical versus nonradical personality.

Rothman and Lichter used the TAT measures of motives to understand more fully the complex and tangled relationship between motivation and ideology, while minimizing the ideological biases of the measures of personality. More specifically, they have empirically examined the idea that the 1960s generation of students and activists was a vanguard in the evolution of a new and better society. The student radicals were heralded by such prophets of the New Left as Charles Reich, Norman O. Brown, and Theodore Rozak as exemplars of this emerging society—what Reich called Consciousness III. In some accounts, such as those of psychologist Kenneth Keniston and sociologist Richard Flacks, the radicals of the 1960s were said to provide the prototypes of a new, healthier, expressive generation of Americans in contrast to the supposed authoritarianism and repression of traditional American society. (For an extensive discussion of this literature, see Rothman and Lichter, 1980, 1982.) In a series of studies of student and adult radicals, however, Rothman and Lichter found that rather than exhibiting the liberating themes, both radical adults and students exhibited marked narcissism (e.g., Rothman and Lichter, 1980, 1982, 1984; Rothman, 1984; Lichter, Rothman, and Lichter, 1986). They found that radical students and adults alike exhibited a higher need for power and, in particular, a higher fear of power than did traditionals or nonradicals (1982, pp. 245, 343). Radicals also display a lower need for achievement than do traditionals, as well as a lower need for affiliation (ibid., p. 343). The implication of Rothman and Lichter's work is that the presence of these motives contributes to political radicalism, while their absence tends to inhibit the development of this radicalism.

One major issue in our analysis of the relationship of the motive scores to ideology among our full sample of elites is the presumed causal direction of the relationship. Does adherence to political attitudes of what we call laissez-faire economic individualism and conservative Victorian morality foster need for achievement, or does the preexisting personality disposition, such as the need for achievement, permit the ethic of rugged individualism to resonate, to seem plausible, and be adopted by the individual as a credo? Or do these develop together, but independently, as part of the larger process of family socialization, education, and career?

We lack the data to resolve the issue definitively, which would require a massive intergenerational panel study, but we explore several different facets of the complex interaction between personality and ideology. Our contention is that both the acquisition of ideological labels (i.e., an ideological identity) and the development of the adult personality (and its dimensions) take place within the family unit of origin over a long period of time. We believe, however, that the adoption of specific issue attitudes is also influenced by external events and institutions such as the media.

We analyze the data in what we believe is the most plausible causal direction—namely, that the growth and development of need dispositions precede the development of ideological views and provide one ground for their acceptability. In this view, one reason for the adoption of ideological views is that they "feel" right; they make explicit and articulate a certain sensibility. Unlike the classic "strain" theories, which Geertz describes and critiques so well (1973, pp. 204–8), we think an elective affinity exists between the growing development of emotional predisposition and the cultural explanation that "fits" this predisposition.

TAT MEASURES OF MOTIVES

The TAT stories are scored to assess a variety of motivations. Psychologists Dan McAdams (1980, 1982) and David Winter and Abigail Stewart (1978) refer to these motives as "affective-toned cognitive cluster(s) that energize, direct, and select behavior and experience in certain situations" (McAdams, 1980, p. 293). These motives, which we sometimes call need dispositions, are most adequately tapped through thematic coding of thought samples in response to neutral stimuli. This neutral picture is the stimulus that triggers these cognitive associations in the telling of the stories (see esp. Winter, 1973, pp. 20–95).

The TATs administered to the elite groups in our study consisted of a set of five photographs of ambiguous social situations. Respondents wrote stories about the individuals depicted in the pictures, prompted by questions about what is occurring in the picture, what led up to the current situation, what the people involved are thinking about, and what the final outcome of the interaction is likely to be.

All of the scoring systems were developed in experimental situations, and a large body of empirical research, conducted over a period of forty years in some cases, indicates that they do accurately indicate several key personality traits (Atkinson, 1958; Winter, 1973; McClelland, 1975; Winter and Stewart, 1978; Cole, 1979; Stewart, 1982; Zeldow, Daugherty, and McAdams, 1988). The TAT motives scores allow us to formulate correlations between patterns of personality and the social and attitudinal factors we have been discussing—that is, separately gathered data on profession, background, and expressed political and social attitudes. Accepting the results of these empirically derived scoring systems requires only the belief that individuals are not always aware of their real motives and that such motives may be tapped effectively by presenting respondents with ambiguous stimuli. The empirical work of McClelland and others provides substantial support for that belief.

TATs are designed to measure differences between groups only, as a matter of statistical probability. Nothing we say about statistical differences in group scores can be reliably applied to individual respondents.[3]

Need for Power

The power motive is measured in terms of the need for power, which is made up of component scores on fear of and hope for power. The methodology for the power analysis derives primarily from the work of McClelland and Winter (McClelland, 1961, 1975; Winter, 1973; Winter and Stewart, 1978), who developed a set of criteria for scoring TATs for power needs. Need for power (*n* Power) is then evaluated by coders trained to recognize certain linguistic expressions showing a concern for power.

For example, Winter's definition of "power imagery" within the stories involves three broad criteria: "someone shows his power concerns through actions which in themselves express his power"; "someone does something that arouses strong positive or negative emotions in others"; and "someone is described as having a concern for his reputation or position." There are several other indicators of power need, such as "prestige of the actor," "stated need for power," "blocks in the world [obstacles]," "goal anticipation," and so on. These factors are combined to yield a composite score, which can then be used to compare groups of people that have been differentiated on other terms (e.g., the movie elite versus the business elite).

The following account, by a movie elite respondent, is a good example of the type of story yielding a high need for power:

> The recruit is thinking that he will have to deal more subtly with the power that faces him. He will have to, perhaps, ingratiate himself with these cretins who wear stripes and bars. He is learning to adjust to the real world rather than to continue to fight it. He is going underground.
>
> He will adjust, perhaps even excel at functioning in the world that he at first abhorred and tried to escape from. In time he will take the place of the steel-eyed superior on the left and even find himself facing a sullen, cowering youth who is rebelling at *his* authority. He will survive, he will prevail, and he will propagate the system that he finds so repellent.

Personalities characterized by high *n* Power scores tend to engage in competitive and contact sports, impulsive aggressive activity (such as public arguments), sexual aggressiveness, and unstable dating and marital relations. Power-oriented people are also attracted to symbols of prestige. With the effects of class differences taken into account, *n* Power predicts ownership of sports cars and a large number of credit cards. High *n* Power people also have a competitive or hostile stand toward those of higher status or power; they seek to dominate low-status individuals. Persons with high power scores can be effective leaders, if their impulse control is good, they do not score too high on a measure of fear of power, and their achievement scores are also robust.

HOPE FOR AND FEAR OF POWER. Hope for power and fear of power are scored according to whether the predominant orientation is approach (hope) or avoidance (fear). Fear of power is scored under three circumstances: "the power goal is for the direct or indirect benefit of another"; "the actor has doubt about his ability to influence, control or impress others"; and "the writer of the story suggests that power is deceptive or has a flaw" (Winter, 1973, pp. 261–63). All stories with power themes not scored for fear of power are scored as exhibiting the hope for power. The overall score of the need for power motive is the sum of the hope and the fear scores (ibid., p. 263).

Persons who score high on fear of power behave in ways that suggest they are afraid of other people gaining power over them. Individuals strongly motivated by fear of power mistrust other people and institutional authority. They are concerned with self and defending their personal autonomy and independence. Thus they find it difficult to cooperate in group activities, or to compete with others, or to take on responsibility in an institutional setting. Paranoid personalities tend to score very high on fear of power (McClelland, 1975; Winter, 1973). Interestingly, scores on stories in which the power goal is the direct or indirect benefit of others seem to bear no relationship to benevolent behavior.

The personality types that simultaneously score high on a need for power and a fear of power rationalize their power needs as required to protect themselves against others whom they think seek power over them. In other words, their very fear of power seems to generate a defensive need to feel powerful. The statistical profile of the personality types who score high on fear of power suggests that they tend to engage often in defensive projection and seek power indirectly, that is, in a manner which avoids having to confront other power-seekers directly.

The following TAT story by a journalist writing about a picture of men in uniform illustrates several facets of the fear of power. The reporter sets the story in World War II Germany. An army recruit, Franz, gets fed up with the Nazis and tries to escape. He is caught by soldiers who suspect he is an American spy. The reporter concludes his story: "The future for Franz looked bleak. Whatever he did—confess the reality or contrive to deny the accusation—would lead to the same end—execution." The authorities are real brutes—Nazis. The outcome of the power relationship will be the protagonist's death. A sense of irony contributes to the despairing tone: either the truth or a lie, for different reasons, will produce equally dreadful consequences. The author could have had Franz escape or lie his way out of the dilemma. His future need not have been so bleak in a story less pervaded by a fear of power.

McClelland found no evidence that, on a personal level, those whose stories are concerned with helping others are any more likely to engage in such help than those whose stories are concerned with increasing their own power.

Need for Achievement

McClelland is perhaps most well-known for his TAT scoring system measuring the need for achievement. It was the first motive for which he developed an empirical scoring system, and its validity has been systematically examined over a relatively long period of time. Achievement studies have shown that groups with high TAT scores in need for achievement are also inclined toward moderate risk-taking and entrepreneurial or managerial success, even in noncapitalist societies. TAT themes are scored for *n* Achievement when stories express a concern about meeting a standard of excellence set for oneself (Atkinson, 1958; McClelland, 1961).

Affiliation and Intimacy

TAT themes are scored for the need for affiliation when the story themes manifest a concern to establish, maintain, or restore a reservoir of self-esteem or a positive affective relationship with another person (Rothman, 1984). McAdams, Rothman, and Lichter (1982, p. 594) characterize the need for affiliation as "feeling liked and having friends," but the need for affiliation also includes the fear of rejection (p. 595) and is sometimes difficult to interpret. We use it here to explore McClelland's authoritarian types, for that is the measure he used and tested empirically.

The need for intimacy was developed in 1980 by psychologist Dan McAdams. It is related to affiliation, but it focuses on a desire for the relationship itself, rather than the sociability, gregariousness, and outgoingness associated with the need for friends and friendship. Intimacy is scored when TAT themes reflect "a surrendering of control in relationships, reciprocal, and non-instrumental interaction with others, concern for the affective warmth and communal harmony of social encounters and a special appreciation for sincere self-disclosure" (McAdams, Rothman, and Lichter, 1982, p. 595). It lacks the approach-avoidance aspects associated with need for power and need for affiliation, but emphasizes strictly the positive approach aspects of the motive.

Inhibition, Sublimation

TAT researchers have also formulated another measure, which assesses the degree to which the power motive is inhibited or sublimated. The number of *nots* a respondent used in the stories she or he writes was found to correlate highly with evidence of inhibition. A high inhibition score indicates a sublimation of power, while a low inhibition score is associated with evidence of a more direct expression of the power drive, including a tendency to anger easily and to engage in impulsive violence (McClelland, 1975). When the mean number of *nots* is subtracted from the *n* Power score it provides a measure of power that controls for accompanying feelings of inhibition.

Authoritarianism

On the basis of their work, McClelland and his co-workers developed a measure of authoritarianism, dividing authoritarian personalities into three types (McClelland, 1975).

THE IMPERIAL TYPE. The imperial type scores high on *n* Power and inhibition and low on *n* Affiliation. This type of person can subordinate his or her power needs to an organization and can, other things being equal, succeed as a certain kind of executive. While unwilling to allow challenges to their own authority, these people govern fairly according to general rules.

People with the imperial motivational pattern act in ways that build strong organizations. They like to be in them, to work for them. They like to work. They share with others out of a sense of obligation to the system. Their concern with justice inclines them to deal with people even-handedly. One should also recall that they also display the kinds of assertiveness (that) characterize men and women with high *n* Power. (McClelland, 1975, pp. 294–95)

THE CONQUISTADOR PERSONALITY. By contrast, a pattern of low inhibition levels in conjunction with high power and low affiliative needs defines a more impulsive, power-oriented mentality. People with this motivational syndrome tend to reject institutional ties and to engage in overtly assertive or self-aggrandizing behavior. They seem willing to achieve heightened power goals by manipulating others, with little concern for their wishes or interests. They may be rebels against authority but their rebellion, however it is rationalized, ultimately serves the cause of self-aggrandizement.

THE PERSONAL ENCLAVE TYPE. People with this third power orientation view the self rather than others as the locus of their efforts to gain feelings of power. They seek to feel powerful by incorporating strength through alliances with people, groups, or ideas they perceive as sources of power. Enclave types are characterized by high n Power, low inhibitions, and high n Affiliation.

Narcissism[4]

Healthy adult narcissism is a reservoir of self-esteem and is an adequate basis of positive self-feeling, while its negative side is responsible for association with selfishness and egoism. People who lack confidence in themselves, who suffer from what psychologists call narcissistic deficits, often rely on egocentric mechanisms to enhance self-esteem and maintain a sense of identity. This leads to behavior commonly termed narcissistic.

One way of enhancing self-esteem and maintaining one's identity is a wishful or grandiose self-image, whereby the narcissist denies the undesirable qualities that he or she perceives in him or herself and projects these traits on others. This devaluation of others also protects the bearer against the feelings of deprivation caused by envy. In general, the narcissistic type uses others primarily to bolster self-esteem and thereby avoids seeing them as separate individuals with needs and identities different from those of the narcissist.

TAT stories characterized by a high degree of narcissism emphasize the gratification of exhibitionistic needs rather than interpersonal issues. These writers appear to be showing off, calling attention to themselves while ignoring any relationship that the story might invoke. Stories characterized by a high degree of narcissism also portray characters as exploitative, haughty, manipulative, grandiose, cold, ruthless, and/or hollow. This reflects the narcissist's tendency to project negative personality traits onto other people and to retain self-esteem by denigrating others.

For example, writing a story about a picture of a man and a woman, a male television news producer offers the classic portrait of an unfeeling seducer: "It has taken him six months to get Larry's wife into bed. Six months of cajoling, soft words, good wine, and, finally, words of love. Words unmeant but believed. Now it was all over. . . . And he wondered, how the hell he would get rid of her." Again, an intuitive reading of this kind of story seems clear enough. The point, however, is that as these stories accumulate and we correlate them with other divisions among the entire sample (journalist-businessman, for example), patterns emerge that allow us to build reliable, statistical profiles.

MOTIVE SCORES AS PREDICTORS OF IDEOLOGY
AND OCCUPATION

If, as we have argued, need disposition is one ground of ideological views, then it should be possible to predict ideological beliefs from prior knowledge of motive scores. The first task in the analysis, then, is to examine the relationship between ideology and the need dispositions. The second task is to treat motive scores as predictors of occupational choice. The intervening variables in the first part become the dependent variables in the second.[5]

Motives as Predictors of Ideology

Table 8.1 presents correlations between motive scores and ideology, both self-defined and in terms of the factors that comprise contemporary liberalism. The need for achievement correlates negatively, but only moderately, with self-identified liberalism. The need for power, the need for affiliation, and the need for intimacy are positively, but again only moderately, related to self-identified liberalism. Neither narcissism nor inhibition seems to play an explanatory role for the dependent variable. Hope and fear of power do, but both correlate so highly with *n* Power itself that they could not be used in the same set of equations, and we excluded them from further analysis.

The relationship between motives and each of the four components of liberalism is even more modest, except for the collectivist liberalism and regime threat dimensions, though far from nugatory. Given the difficulties of tapping psychological characteristics, the results are not without importance. It is also at least possible that combining the four factors into a single additive liberalism scale would produce more robust results.

Using a stepwise regression to measure the independent explanatory power of personality produces even less robust results. The only motives that achieve statistical significance as predictors for any of the components of ideology are achievement, which correlates negatively with alienation and regime threat; the need for power, which correlates positively with collectivist liberalism and regime threat (essentially a measure of alienation); and the desire for intimacy, which correlates only with regime threat. None of the motives is even a statistically significant predictor of self-defined ideology. The weakness of the relationship prevents us from attempting to explain much by referring to psychological variables, although we must note two caveats. First, combining the ideo-

TABLE 8.1 Correlations of Psychological Motives and Measures of Ideology

Motive	Need for Power	Hope for Power	Fear of Power	Need for Intimacy	Need for Affiliation	Inhibition	Narcissism	Ideology	Alienation	Expressive Individualism	Collective Liberalism	Regime Threat
Need for achievement	0.15	0.00	0.18	0.08	0.05	0.05	-0.06	-0.13	-0.05	-0.02	-0.09	-0.09
Need for power		0.71	0.53	0.07	0.23	0.16	0.05	0.14	0.05	0.06	0.13	0.10
Hope for power			-0.22	0.16	0.21	0.12	-0.04	0.11	0.02	-0.01	0.11	0.04
Fear of power				0.06	0.06	0.05	0.09	0.07	0.09	0.09	0.07	0.12
Need for intimacy					0.62	0.12	-0.12	0.12	0.06	-0.02	0.10	0.09
Need for affiliation						0.16	0.07	0.09	0.06	-0.04	0.09	0.05
Inhibition							0.00	0.04	-0.01	0.03	0.02	0.10
Narcissism								0.00	0.05	0.07	0.00	0.06

logical factors into one scale would probably, given their common direc-
tionality, yield statistically significant results. Second, and at least as
important, it is possible that the personality effects are mediated by other
variables, primarily by occupation, which is a fairly robust predictor of
ideology. After all, occupational choices are generally made years after
people develop stable personalities. It has long been accepted that psychological motives do impact on occupational choice. The argument is
made more persuasive given the large differences in the ideological
scores of members of various occupations (see Table 8.2).

Occupation Ideology and Personality

To clarify the relationship between personality and occupation we
relied on a discriminant analysis comparing business elites with the three
cultural elites included in our sample (film, television, and journalism
elites; see Tables 8.3 and 8.4). We included the other significant predictors of occupation in the equation. Rothman's goal, in the overall study of
which this book is part, has always been to emphasize this comparison.
The hypotheses that have guided this work were drawn partly from the
work of Daniel Bell (see Rothman and Lichter, 1984; Rothman, 1992a).
The cultural elites, in Bell's theory, mount the critical attack on the
bourgeois sensibility that has traditionally defined the American experience.

The hypotheses were borne out. Motives are among the best predictors of occupation of those questions we used for this purpose. Power
and achievement scores are among the strongest predictors of this occupational difference, along with education and not being Jewish.[6] The
latter relationship reflects the quite large proportion of the cultural elites
who are of Jewish background as compared with the business elite. Thus
the cultural elites' occupational choice, and to some extent their ideology
(more liberal than that of the business elite), correlates positively with
higher power, narcissism, and intimacy scores and negatively with
achievement scores.[7] The cultural elites score substantially higher on
regime threat and expressive individualism measures of ideology and on
the indicated motives. While their inhibition scores are higher in absolute terms than those of the business elite, they are not higher than the
differences in power needs between the two groups.

Finally, the new cultural elites are more likely to be authoritarians, as
defined by McClelland, than are business elites. The difference is spread
among the various types of authoritarians, but is most substantial for the
enclave and imperial types (Table 8.5).

TABLE 8.2   Relative Influence of Motives on Self-Labeled Political View (standardized regression weights)

	Criterion				
Predictor	Self-labeled Ideology	Alienation	Expressive Individualism	Collective Liberalism	Regime Threat
Motive					
Intimacy	0.05	0.03	0.01	0.02	0.06*
Achievement	−0.03	−0.05*	−0.02	−0.02	−0.11*
Power	0.04	0.01	0.03	0.06*	0.09*
Occupation					
Bureaucrats	−0.05	−0.13*	−0.13*	−0.01	−0.14*
Business	−0.22*	−0.13*	−0.16*	−0.17*	
Congressional aides	−0.05	−0.10*	−0.14*	−0.01	−0.15*
Judges	−0.05	−0.12*	−0.15*	0.04	−0.01
Labor	0.07*	0.04	−0.13*	0.14*	−0.08*
Lawyers	−0.08*	−0.23*	−0.06	−0.05	−0.05
Media	−0.04	−0.07	0.00	−0.08*	
Military	−0.23*	−0.13*	−0.27*	−0.12*	−0.39*
Movies	0.03	0.06	−0.01	0.02	
Public interest	0.13*	0.11*	−0.04	0.21*	
Religious leaders	−0.04	0.02	−0.32	−0.13	0.01
Father's view	0.22*	0.04	−0.32*	0.13*	0.01
Father's socioeconomic status	0.00	0.01	0.04*	0.02	0.02
Race	0.06*	0.138	0.02	0.05*	0.01
Sex	0.08*	0.08*	0.12*	0.02	0.09*
Religious affiliation					
Catholic	−0.10*	−0.04	−0.30*	−0.02	−0.05
Protestant	−0.14*	−0.10*	−0.15*	−0.06*	−0.10*
Jewish	0.02	0.01	−0.02	0.06*	−0.06*
**Region					
South	−0.04	−0.04	0.00	−0.05*	−0.05
Midwest	−0.03	−0.02	−0.03	−0.03	−0.02
West	−0.03	−0.03	−0.02	−0.02	0.00
Foreign born	0.03	−0.04*	0.04	−0.02	−0.02

(continued)

TABLE 8.2 (*Continued*)

			Criterion		
Predictor	*Self-labeled Ideology*	*Alienation*	*Expressive Individualism*	*Collective Liberalism*	*Regime Threat*
Education	0.04	−0.11*	0.04	−0.08*	0.21*
Age	0.06*	−0.07*	0.02	0.03	0.04
R-squared	0.32*	0.24*	0.34*	0.24*	0.27*
Change in R-squared	0.0040	0.0022	0.0007	0.0029	0.0164
N	1,862	1,852	1,862	1,852	931

*Significant at $p < 0.05$.
Change in R-squared indicates the independent contribution of the motives.
**For each set of categorical predictors, such as occupation or region, one category is treated as the reference group. In this case, the regression weights represent the difference between each of the other regions and the Northeast.

Table 8.3   Demographics and Psychological Motives as Predictors of Differences Between Business and New Cultural Elites (standardized discriminant weights)

	Weight
Education	0.45
Father's view	−0.19
Age	0.10
Not Jewish	0.52
Father's socioeconomic status	0.29
Motives	
Achievement	0.49
Intimacy	0.01
Narcissism	0.07
Power	−0.30
Explained variance	0.16*
Group means	
Business elite	0.83
New cultural elites	0.18

$N = 652$
*Significant at $p < 0.05$.

TABLE 8.4   Mean Scores on the Motives and Ideological Dimensions
for Business and New Cultural Elites

	Business Elite	New Cultural Elite
Achievement	8.30	5.66
Intimacy	2.82	3.35
Narcissism	20.56	21.48
Power	6.05	7.80
Fear of power	2.56	3.14
Inhibition	2.68	2.82
Self-defined ideology	2.96	4.38
Alienation	95.34	96.42
Expressive individualism	92.14	100.22
Collective liberalism	93.56	99.50
Regime threat	90.86	100.35

DISCUSSION

The need for achievement and the need for power have effects on both
political liberalism and more powerfully on career choice. The greater
the need for achievement, the more conservative an individual is likely to
be, the more likely he or she is to be a member of the business elite, and
the less likely he or she is to be a member of the cultural elites. Further,
the greater the need for power, the more likely a respondent is politically
liberal, the less likely a business leader, and the more likely to choose a
career in one of the newer elite occupations. The same pattern of career
choice is associated with higher scores on measures of narcissistic pathology and the desire for intimacy.

The relationship seems paradoxical. The search for power would
appear to exclude intimacy as a goal. Certainly one of the characteristics

TABLE 8.5   Frequencies of the Authoritarian Types for
Business and New Cultural Elites (percentage)

	Business Elite	New Cultural Elite
Not authoritarian	81.8	68.3
Authoritarian	18.2	31.7
Authoritarian type (% of total)		
Imperial	5.4	8.4
Conquistador	10.7	12.9
Enclave	2.1	10.4
N	249	596

of narcissistic personality types is their inability to develop intimate relations with others. As McAdams, the creator of the intimacy scale, notes, those who score high in both the need for power and the need for intimacy tend to be emotionally troubled (1982, 1988, 1989). While McAdams has not scored for narcissism, it is not unreasonable to suggest that the moderately high intimacy scores of the cultural elites reflect their inability to develop genuine intimacy with another person.

Although it is to be expected from McClelland's work that the need for achievement is positively related to business choice, it may be surprising that membership in the business elite is negatively related to the need for power. This result fits, however, with the view of such social commentators as Joseph Schumpeter (1950), Daniel Bell (1978), and Irving Kristol (1978). Business leaders do not desire power over other people but prefer a field of action that permits them to achieve excellence. As McClelland (1961) points out, accomplishment in business is not mere materialism. Successful businesspeople interpret monetary rewards as proof of this excellence. Kristol observes that the original Horatio Alger novels develop the theme that the business life is a good life because it allows the development of certain character traits: "probity, diligence, thrift, self-reliance, self-respect, candor, fair dealing"—in short, the middle class, bourgeois, Victorian virtues (1978, p. 81). Kristol goes on to suggest that business is no longer the repository of such virtues and hopes. He may well be right, but our data show that businessmen and women are still more likely to be characterized by such orientations than are the cultural elites.

NINE

CONCLUSION: DIVIDED ELITES, AMERICAN SOCIETY, AND SOCIAL CHANGE

The image of a unified American elite, a commonplace of the 1950s, is of limited relevance today. If it was once a cohesive caste, it is no longer. Some of the cultural divisions are the result of greater diversity of background among American elites; only a plurality are Anglo-Saxon Protestants, although most members of American elites are overwhelmingly white and male.[1] A significant proportion of their fathers were not upper-status white-collar professionals or managers, but lower white- and blue-collar workers such as shopkeepers, salesmen, clerical workers, and laborers. While almost all graduated from college, many did not go to America's most prestigious schools. In other words, American elites are leaders only because they are members in one or another key group. They are defined as members of the elite, above all, by their occupations.

Our study demonstrates how divided American elites really are. We explored the multiple dimensions of American ideology as exhibited by American elites. Our extensive analysis of the familial sources of current beliefs revealed that politicized families pass down political labels and through them, in part, occupational choices to their children. All other things being equal, liberal parents do not usually raise children to be business and military leaders, but do raise the kind of person likely to become a public interest group leader or a member of one of the elite cultural groups. Parental views interact with occupational socialization to create a climate supportive of certain views rather than others.

It seems to us that the most ideological persons are those who take on the label liberal or conservative from their parents. They then absorb the proper mix of political attitudes that fit the label. In addition, the multidimensional nature of ideology shows that persons frequently are liberal on issues such as collectivist liberalism but are conservative on other issues. Religious elites and labor leaders fit this ideological picture. In fact, being a labor leader has an independent effect on collectivist liberalism, along with having a liberal father, being better educated, and being Jewish.

Conversely, many in the media, movies, and television are supportive of issues of expressive individualism. Here again, however, the expressive individualism associated with the cultural elite is also associated with numerous other social background factors: gender, education, being either secular or Jewish, and/or having a liberal mother.

The adversary culture, in its purest form, is found in the conjoining of two ideological dimensions: alienation and regime threat. In both cases, liberal fathers seem to have played a key role. The two factors of system alienation and regime threat seem to structure an individual's worldview more than any other dimension. They are, for example, more significantly related to the reliability ratings of the *National Review, Commentary,* the *Nation,* and the *New York Review of Books,* and to approval ratings of Fidel Castro and the Sandinistas.

We also found distinctive personality motives to be related to political liberalism. The need for achievement is inversely related to political liberalism, while an increasing need for power is related to increasing political liberalism. We examined the business and cultural elites and their constellation of motives to see if career choice is partly a function of personality and mediates its relation to ideology. Persons with stronger needs for achievement are more likely to have chosen a business career. Conversely, a weaker need for achievement is related to a career in the cultural sphere. Those with stronger power needs and higher fear of power scores are more likely to become part of the cultural elite, while a weaker need for power is associated with choosing business as a career. Cultural elites especially are characterized by higher scores in narcissistic pathology and relatively low power/inhibition ratios.

Elite members of new occupations (such as public interest groups), which Irving Kristol and others call the new class, choose these careers and their political ideas as a function of their past. Needless to say, the same is true for elites in traditional sectors. Business leaders go into business at least partially because they come from conservative households, they hold their particular political views, and they have distinctive personality constellations; they come to label themselves conservative.

In other words, political labels are highly charged with personality constellations and moral connotations for American elites. Members of the American elite take specific issue positions to remain consistent with their self-labels. The primacy of matching issue position with ideological label consequently gives tremendous power to those who define what issue position is conservative and what issue position is liberal—that is, American intellectuals. They are found in the universities and colleges, policy think-tanks, media, government, and various social movements. Their ideas are spread by our cultural institutions: the media, movies, television, primary and secondary education, book and magazine publishing, and academia.

American intellectuals, however, are overwhelmingly adversarial toward the American system. The dominant institutions that transmit their values are predominantly liberal and often also adversarial. In any case, conservatives in these occupations are vastly outnumbered.

This brings us back to the role of intellectuals in modern America. Modern intellectuals pride themselves on their anti-Americanism. Structurally, however, adversary culture intellectuals until the 1960s existed outside modern American institutions, with the exception of some prominent academics at the elite universities.[2]

The process of modern role institutionalization has finally caught up with intellectuals. The sixties marked the unprecedented growth of universities and colleges nationwide. This in turn meant the absorption and eventual tenure of large numbers of the New Left cohort, a few of the most prominent including Angela Davis, Todd Gitlin, Richard Flacks, Derek Shearer, and Johnetta Cole (Hollander, 1992, p. 152).

Ideologically, an increasing percentage of academics define themselves as liberal or left-wing. The proportion of conservative academics has remained relatively stable in recent years. The percentage of moderates, however, has declined, while the proportion of liberals has grown. In 1972, 49 percent of academics defined themselves as either liberal or left-wing; 26 percent were moderates, and 25 percent were either moderately or strongly conservative (data are from Ladd and Lipset, 1975, and Hollander, 1992). By 1989, 57 percent called themselves either liberal or moderately liberal, while 27 percent labeled themselves conservative.

Changes in humanities and social science faculties are especially striking. Fifty-four percent of social scientists and 64 percent of humanities faculty were liberal in the 1970s. By 1989, roughly 70 percent of academics in the social sciences and humanities were liberal. In the 1970s, roughly one in five social scientists was conservative, compared with 15 percent by 1989. Twenty-nine percent of humanities professors in the 1970s called themselves conservative, compared with only 18 percent in 1989. Although these data are not available by age and rank, we surmise that almost all the conservatives are professors near retirement, while their younger colleagues are almost uniformly on the left.

More significantly, tenure within universities and colleges, faculty self-governance and academic freedom, and the lack of a mandatory retirement age will shelter members of this ex-New Left cohort within academia. Tenure provides them with permanent employment. Faculty self-governance protects them from administrative, alumni, and public sanction. The lack of mandatory retirement means these professors and their like-minded younger associates will be a part of the academy until they die. Moreover, unlike the media, the movies, television, and publishing, the usual forces of free markets, politics, and public opinion have relatively little impact on tenured faculty (e.g., Kimball, 1990).

The influence of the adversary culture in academia is reflected in the growth and spread of the issue of political correctness. Although the literature on this subject is so voluminous that it is difficult to keep up, some aspects require a brief statement (D'Souza, 1990; Searle, 1990; Hentoff, 1992). Historian Stanley Coben (1991) points out that before the late nineteenth century, American colleges and universities were citadels of religious and political orthodoxy. The growth and spread of the German model of a graduate research university, first established at Johns Hopkins in 1876 and later implemented at Chicago in 1892 and at Columbia and Harvard around the same time, broke the mold of conformity to Victorian values. The research university itself and the academic freedom that makes it possible, however, depend for their support on the assumption that objective truth exists and that it is discoverable by logical argument and empirical research. The growth of the 1960s counterculture, in a frenzy of romantic antirationalism, again broke the mold. It was only a matter of time before a new orthodoxy would be enforced to enjoin conformity with the new adversarial ethos.

Critics of popular culture such as Michael Medved argue that the makers of popular culture identify with the "myth of the alienated artist" (1992, p. 300). We believe other new elite groups, such as public interest leaders and the media elite, identify with the similar myth of the alienated intellectual. Public opinion and American prosperity (which we think is a product of American capitalism) enable such persons to engage in their "new class" occupations. But as Kristol remarks, it is ironic that in a society where business plays such an important role, "there are people out there who find it convenient to believe the worst about business because they have certain adverse intentions toward the business community to begin with. They dislike business for what it is, not for what they mistakenly think it is" (1978, p. 25). If Hollander is right, since the sixties many alienated intellectuals have also come to hate America and all things American, not just the free market and the business class. In turn, conservative groups (especially conservative Christian groups) and conservative intellectuals (the counter to the counterculture) have become their demonized adversaries and *vice versa*.

These findings resonate with the commonly held view that there exists something of a culture war, or at least a Kultur-Kampf, or cultural struggle, among opposing members of the American elite. While various conflicts stemming from this opposition are fought in many different locales, its primary focus is the future direction of the country. It is a conflict between deeply held, sharply antagonistic worldviews or ideologies. If, as we argue, that ideology is itself both a reflection and a further development of a contested culture, then ours is a luxuriantly ideological era. And it is not likely to vanish soon.

Furthermore, the evidence lends credence to the argument that the cultural elite is characterized by personality constellations that may be less compatible with an ordered democratic society than the more traditional motivational patterns characteristic of the business elite. Given the influence of the cultural elites on the culture at large, they may, ironically, be contributing to the undermining of those societal characteristics that have enabled them to live relatively well in the past. In short, we may be moving toward a world increasingly characterized by narcissistic demands, lack of impulse control, and the kind of self-centered suspiciousness that inhibits effective cooperation for common purposes.[3]

APPENDIX

THE INTERVIEW SAMPLE
AND
QUESTIONNAIRE

1. Sample

Bureaucrats. High-ranking bureaucrats make up the sample from the Office of Personnel Management's *List of Senior Executive Personnel*. Political appointees are excluded. Half the sample is drawn from "activist" agencies, which included: the Civil Rights Division of the Justice Department, Environmental Protection Agency, Housing and Urban Development, Federal Trade Commission, Action, Consumer Products Safety Commission, Equal Employment Opportunity Commission, and Health and Human Services. The other half were from "traditional" agencies: Commerce, Agriculture, Treasury, Immigration and Naturalization Services, and the Bureau of Prisons. Interviews were conducted in 1982, with a response rate of 85 percent. The final sample size is 200.

The Business Elite. Upper and middle management personnel were randomly drawn from the official company lists of four Fortune 500 companies and of one firm in each category of *Fortune* lists of the fifty leading retail outlets, banks, and public utilities. As a requirement for cooperation, the names of the corporations cannot be publicly disclosed. Interviews were conducted in 1979. The response rate was 96 percent; the final sample size is 242.

Congressional Aides. The random sample of congressional aides is drawn from key committee and personal staff listed in the *Washington Monitor's 1982 Congressional Yellow Book* and cross-checked with the *Congressional Staff Directory.* The interviews were conducted in 1982, with a response rate of 71 percent. The final sample size is 134.

Federal Judges. The random sample of federal judges consists of those on the bench as of February 1982. Ten at the appeal level and ten district judges were randomly selected from each chosen circuit. The first subsample from New York, Chicago, Los Angeles, and Washington, DC, were interviewed in 1984; the second subsample from Dallas–Ft. Worth, Detroit, St. Louis, San Francisco, Minneapolis–St. Paul, and North Carolina were interviewed in 1985. The response rate for all samples was 54 percent; the final sample size is 114.

Labor Union Leaders. The random sample consists of presidents and secretary treasurers from national unions and trade associations with one thousand or more members, and presidents, vice-presidents, research directors, and business managers of major locals, based on the U.S. Department of Labor's *Directory of National Unions and Employee Associations* and subsequently updated through phone calls. There are two subsamples, one from Washington, DC, New York, Chicago, and Los Angeles done in 1984, the second from Detroit and Minneapolis–St. Paul in 1985. The response rate was 54 percent, the final sample size is 95.

Corporate Lawyers. The random sample of elite corporate lawyers consists of partners from New York and Washington, DC, law firms with more than fifty partners, based on the *Martindale-Hubbell Law Directory.* Interviews were conducted in 1982. The response rate was 66 percent; the final sample size is 150.

The Media Elite. The media sample consists of a random sample of journalists and editors from the *New York Times,* the *Washington Post,* the *Wall Street Journal, Time, Newsweek, U.S. News and World Report,* and the news organizations at NBC, ABC, CBS, and PBS. The sampling frame was derived from internal phone directories and the names of individuals listed on mastheads in the case of news magazines. Staff members with responsibility for news coverage were chosen in consultation with knowledgeable people. A computer-generated random sample was chosen from this pool of names. Interviews were conducted in 1979. The response rate was 74 percent; the final sample size is 238.

The Military Elite. The military elite are a random sample of field-grade officers from the Pentagon phone book and from the class roster of the National Defense University (NDU). The Pentagon sample consists of general and flag-grade officers; the NDU sample consists of noncivilian students mostly at the rank of colonel, commander, and higher. Interviews were conducted in 1982. The response rate was 77 percent; the final sample size is 152.

The Movie Elite. The random sample is drawn from a list of writers, producers, and directors of the fifty top-grossing films made between 1965 and 1982, based on data in *Variety.* Interviews were conducted in 1982. The response rate was 64 percent; the final sample size is 96.

The Public Interest Elite. The random sample is drawn from lists of presidents and members of boards of directors of formal lobbying groups, based on *Public Interest Profiles, Washington Five,* and the *Encyclopedia of Associations;* and lists of attorneys in public interest law firms, drawn from *Public Interest Law: Five Years Later* and *Balancing the Scales of Justice.* Knowledgeable individuals were also consulted. Equal numbers were drawn from lobby groups and public interest law firms and restricted to Washington, DC, and New York City. Interviews were conducted in 1982. The response rate was 84 percent; the final sample size is 158.

Religious Elite. To find the most influential religious leaders, we contacted the leaders of Christian denominations with one million or more members and the editors of leading religious periodicals, such as *Christian Century* (we used their published list of the most influential religious leaders of 1982) and *Christianity and Crisis,* and asked them to nominate the most influential American religious figures. We asked them to include the leading figures from the major Christian denominations, leaders of religiously based social action groups, editors of religious journals, and theologians. These nominees provided the basis of our sample. Names that appeared on multiple lists were included in our preliminary listing, which was sent out to many of the aforementioned groups and individuals for further review. Once again, only consensual choices were retained in our final sample. Among our respondents were the heads of Protestant churches and Catholic orders, university and seminary presidents, editors of major religious publications, prominent "television evangelists," and individuals in leadership positions in such organizations as the National Council of Churches, the Moral Majority, the National Conference of Catholic Bishops, the Religious Roundtable, and the National Association of Evangelicals. The interviewing was conducted in 1984 and 1985. The response rate was 77 percent; the final sample size is 178.

The Television Elite. The television sample is based on a reputational sampling frame of an initial list of 350 writers, producers, and executives associated with the development of two or more successful prime-time television series. Interviews were conducted in 1982. The response rate was 60 percent; the final sample size is 104.

The interviewing firms are: Response Analysis Corporation, Princeton; Metro Research, Washington, DC; Depth Research, New York; Carol Davis Research, Los Angeles; Joyner Hutcheson Researchers, Atlanta; Arlene Fine Associates, Chicago; Davideen Swanger, Dallas; High Scope Research, Detroit; Quality Control Services, Minneapolis–St. Paul; Bartlett Research, San Francisco; and Field Service, Inc., St. Louis. All interviewers were employees of the firms and received special training, orientation seminars, and preliminary practice interviews. Response Analysis supervised the pretesting of the original questionnaire.

2. Questions Asked of Elite Groups

Questions Asked of Twelve-Group Sample

V142   Less government regulation of business would be good for the country.

V143   The American legal system mainly favors the wealthy.

V144   The American private enterprise system is generally fair to working people.

V145   It is a woman's right to decide whether or not to have an abortion.

V147   It is not the proper role of government to insure that everyone has a job.

V148   Under a fair economic system, people with more ability should earn higher salaries.

V149   Lesbians and homosexuals should not be allowed to teach in public schools.

V151   Our environmental problems are not as serious as people have been led to believe.

V152   The government should work to substantially reduce the income gap between the rich and the poor.

V153   The United States needs a complete restructuring of its basic institutions.

V154   Big corporations should be taken out of private ownership and run in the public interest.

V157   The structure of our society causes most people to feel alienated.

V158   It is wrong for a married person to have sexual relations with someone other than his or her spouse.

V159   It is wrong for adults of the same sex to have sexual relations.

V160   The United States has a moral obligation to prevent the destruction of Israel.

V161   It is sometimes necessary for the CIA to protect U.S. interests by undermining hostile governments.

V163   The main goal of U.S. foreign policy has been to protect U.S. business interests.

Additional Questions Asked of Eight-Group Sample

V166   We should be more forceful in our dealings with the Soviet Union even if it increases the risk of war.

V167   Special preference in hiring should be given to blacks.

V168   Special preference in hiring should be given to women.

V171   Hard work will always pay off if you have faith in yourself and stick to it.

V175   In general, people are poor because of circumstances beyond their control rather than lack of effort.

V176   In general, blacks don't have the chance for the education it takes to rise out of poverty.

V177   In general, blacks don't have the motivation or willpower to pull themselves out of poverty.

V178   Almost all the gains made by blacks in recent years have come at the expense of whites.

V184   The government ought to make sure everyone has a good standard of living.

V185   It is important for America to have the strongest military force in the world, no matter what it costs.

V186   A woman with young children should not work outside the home unless it is financially necessary.

V187   The U.S. would be better off if it moved toward socialism.

V188   There is too much concern in the courts for the rights of criminals.

The questions asked of the elite groups are all in Likert scale format (strongly agree, agree, disagree, strongly disagree). The eight groups are bureaucrats, military, public interest leaders, lawyers, congressional aides, religious leaders, judges, and labor union leaders.

3. Questions Loading on Each Factor

Factor 1. System Alienation

V143   The American legal system mainly favors the wealthy.

V144   The American private enterprise system is generally fair to working people.

V153   The United States needs a complete restructuring of its basic institutions.

V154   Big corporations should be taken out of private ownership and run in the public interest.

V157   The structure of our society causes most people to feel alienated.

V163   The main goal of U.S. foreign policy has been to protect U.S. business interests.

Factor 2. Expressive Individualism

V145   It is a woman's right to decide whether or not to have an abortion.

V149   Lesbians and homosexuals should not be allowed to teach in public schools.

V158   It is wrong for a married person to have sexual relations with someone other than his or her spouse.

V159   It is wrong for adults of the same sex to have sexual relations.

Factor 3. Collectivist Liberalism

V142   Less government regulation of business would be good for the country.

V147   It is not the proper role of government to insure that everyone has a job.

V151   Our environmental problems are not as serious as people have been led to believe.

V152   The government should work to substantially reduce the income gap between the rich and the poor.

NOTES

Preface

1. The only recent study that approximates our work is that of Verba and Orren (1985).

Chapter 1: The Few Versus the Many

1. Aristotle's democracy and polity, based on rule by the many, are an exception.

2. Details of the sample are provided in the appendix.

3. Recent controversy over allowing homosexuals in the military reflects this conflict of values.

4. Today they would include CNN. When the study was conducted the cable news network was not yet an important player. There are those who argue that, given the proliferation of television channels, the era of nationalization is now over, and that, increasingly, particular channels will cater not to local interests but to different racial, ethnic, and religious groups. (See the series of articles in *Society,* July/August 1993.)

Chapter 2: Room at the Top

1. These statistics are as of 1985.

2. No doubt popular music elite members would have even less education.

3. The selectivity of the undergraduate institution attended was measured by the same index used by Ladd and Lipset (1975) in their study of university and college professors. This index rates the quality of undergraduate colleges on several criteria, including the quality of the faculty, selectivity of student admission, and size of the institution's endowment. These figures were combined to produce a single measure of quality. They were then divided into a seven-point scale ranging from a score of one, which is the lowest possible score, to a score of seven, which is the highest possible score. "Highly selective," "elite school," and "best" are used here as synonymous terms indicating a score of seven.

4. This does not mean that such discrimination no longer exists. Of course it does, although the costs of openly violating the law are far greater than they ever used to be.

5. We are speaking of the years 1980 to 1984. We suspect that this has substantially changed in the past ten to fifteen years.

6. Dye's study of elites (1986) differs somewhat from ours primarily because he focuses on who occupies what leadership position, their social backgrounds, and interlocking civic and corporate ties (pp. 9–13). Dye does not conduct an independent survey of elites and thus lacks data on their fundamental values and worldview. One of his primary sources of data is Rothman and Lichter's findings on the media, movie, television, public interest, and business elites (quoted in Dye, 1986, pp. 237–39).

7. The miscellaneous category consists of occupations we could not classify, such as military, gambler, and so on.

Chapter 3: The Structure of Ideology

1. The process produces greater cohesion within specific occupational spheres and at the same time decreases unity between them. Although an extended discussion of this point is beyond the scope of the chapter, one manifestation of this elite fragmentation is the disappearance of generalized "wise men" leaders, as chronicled by sociologists such as Digby Baltzell (1979).

2. There is no agreement among its proponents, however, as to the causes of or the prognosis for the adversary culture.

3. See, for example, Davis, 1980; Ladd, 1979; Brint, 1984. Macy (1988) provides an interesting neo-Marxian explanation critical of new class theories which is tested by means of a complex statistical model. He concludes that "the growth of the extra-market economy [provides] the structural basis of opposition to business" (p. 348).

4. Geertz provides the joke (1973, p. 194).

5. Sociologist Edward Shils's contrast between "ideology" and "civility," in his discussion of McCarthyism (1956), is a perfect example of the pejorative usage. Our disagreement with him is not normative, for the kind of totalist ideology he condemns is a threat to the existence of free society. Rather, we believe that it is analytically more fruitful to begin with a nonpejorative concept of ideology.

6. In chapter eight, we examine the psychological correlates of ideology, following the approach set forth in Rothman and Lichter's *Roots of Radicalism* (1982).

7. This hypothesis appears to fit the emergence of the two wings of contemporary American political culture quite well. Roughly speaking, modern American progressivist liberalism emerged as a reaction to the laissez-faire capitalism of the Gilded Age with its cycles of prosperity and depression, and its increasing disparities between wealth and poverty (e.g., Goldman, 1952; Lerner, Nagai, and Rothman, 1995, chap. 2). Modern American conservatism is an even more recent outgrowth. It arose in response to the success of the New Deal in institutionalizing itself as the preeminent American political tradition (e.g., Nash, 1976). Once the ideologies are successfully established as ongoing traditions of thought and action, of course, they take on an independent existence.

8. Ironically, the rise of "neo-conservatism" has changed that state of affairs somewhat, for it has changed the character of conservative cadres. The change is illustrated by the emergence of a number of new conservative magazines, the first of which was Irving Kristol's *The Public Interest*. Of course, in absolute numbers liberal and radical intellec-

tuals still outnumber conservatives by a large margin as the Carnegie Foundation's studies of the professoriate demonstrate.

9. One can draw a parallel between our procedure for analyzing political liberalism and that used by psychologists to understand intelligence. Just as psychologists recognize a general concept of intelligence while simultaneously distinguishing between verbal, mathematical, abstract, and spatial reasoning, we believe that the phenomenon of ideology cannot be properly understood without considering ideology to be a multidimensional construct, even though for some purposes a single measure is adequate. Needless to say, we consider ideology to be a purely cultural and social construct, and the analysis of ideology is in no way as advanced as that of intelligence.

10. We replicated the complete factor analysis on an independent sample of the philanthropy elite. We found the same four factors as here, with an identical pattern of factor loadings and score coefficients (Nagai, Lerner, and Rothman, 1994).

11. It should not be necessary to say so in a book of this kind, but given previous reactions to our work, we emphasize that defining expressive individualism as an ideology implies no moral stance on it or any of its components. We are describing an ideology in the sense that Geertz uses the term.

12. Not all questions loaded on the factors. In particular, the Israel question never loaded on any factor in either analysis and, more surprisingly, neither did the question about the able earning more. While the question on CIA overthrows also failed to load on the first factor analysis, it did load on the outside threat factor. A final point of interest is that the alienation factor obtained from the second factor analysis contained all the questions of the first with the significant addition of the question on the desirability of the United States moving toward socialism, which loaded strongly on this expanded alienation factor. The loading confirms the meaning we have assigned to the system alienation factor as distinct from the collectivist liberalism factor.

13. This issue has been the subject of considerable debate. In a well-known article, Kinder and Sears (1981) asserted that opposition to affirmative action and busing constituted a form of symbolic racism. They were sharply criticized by Sniderman and Tetlock (1986), and the debate has continued. Indeed, *Political Psychology* for September 1994 contained several articles on the issue, each with extensive references. It seems to us that Tetlock and Sniderman win hands down.

14. Traditionally, those holding conservative views on this dimension are described as punitive or authoritarian by social scientists, while those holding more liberal views are seen as benign or at least as perceiving the outside world as benign. Further analysis, however, raises some questions about such labels. Scoring low on regime threat correlates with support for Fidel Castro and the Sandinistas (in the 1980s) as well as a fear of power. These data suggest that such individuals have latent positive attitudes toward persons who attack the regime, even if the latter are criminals and certainly if they are revolutionaries.

15. Divisions occur within occupations also. Thus, 71 percent of the congressional aides who work for the Democrats are liberals compared with 29 percent of those who work for the Republicans. Similarly, 80 percent of mainline Protestant religious leaders, 59 percent of Catholic leaders, and 14 percent of fundamentalist religious leaders call themselves liberal.

16. Not only is the overall F test statistically significant at better than the $p < 0.0001$ level of significance, but so are many of the individual pairwise comparisons. We calcu-

lated these values using the Scheffe technique of simultaneous confidence intervals (e.g., Neter, Wasserman, and Whitmore, 1973). It assumes a 5 percent level of significance for any pairwise comparison, taking into account that the use of multiple tests is likely to turn up significant results by chance alone.

In addition, Democratic congressional aides average 101.37, while Republican aides average 95.77. Similarly, we found that Roman Catholic leaders average 104.92, mainline Protestants average 105.58, while fundamentalist Protestant leaders average 96.54.

17. We found that Democratic congressional aides have an average alienation score of 101.37, while Republican aides have a score of 96.46. Roman Catholic leaders have an average system alienation score of 103.44, mainline Protestants 104.35, and fundamentalist Protestant leaders 100.55.

18. The difference between Republican and Democratic congressional aides on expressive individualism is not especially great. Republicans average 98.65, while Democrats average 100.44. The differences among religious leaders, however, are large, and those between religious leaders and members of the cultural elite are profound. Roman Catholic leaders average 88.95, mainline Protestants average 95.76, while fundamentalist leaders average 85.74. The difference between fundamentalist leaders and the liberal cluster of public interest leaders, filmmakers, television creators, and media elite is equal to two standard deviations. On issues of expressive individualism, these groups are extremely divergent.

19. There are modest differences between Republican congressional aides at 96.11 and Democratic aides at 99.39.

20. The simple correlation between self-identified liberalism and system alienation is 0.41. With collectivist liberalism it is 0.61, with regime threat it is 0.53, with expressive individualism it is 0.33. All these correlations are statistically significant at the $p < 0.0001$ level or better.

Chapter 4: Four Dimensions of Ideology and Their Impact

1. We have scored regime threat so that the lower the score received, the more one sees various outsider groups as threats to the public order.

2. We used the method of common factors and extracted all factors with eigenvalues greater than one. We employed a varimax rotation and used the regression method of computing factor scores for new variables.

3. For each goal, the level of statistical significance is $p < 0.0001$ level or better. When goals were recoded into two categories, materialist goals and postmaterialist goals, the difference between support for materialist values and postmaterialist values is also statistically significant. Choices of second goals and choices of least important goals (not shown here) follow the same pattern and are also statistically significant. Lastly, the differences for self-identified liberalism are strong and statistically significant.

4. This is due to the resulting heteroscedasticity (nonconstancy) in the variance of the error terms, which invalidates the significance tests (e.g., Hanushek and Jackson, 1977).

5. Discriminant analysis is a member of the generalized linear model, to which ordinary least squares (OLS) regression also belongs. A linear combination of the predictors is calculated to maximize discrimination—that is, assignment of cases into groups. There are potentially $N - 1$ discriminant functions for a set of data, where N is the number of groups (this is true only when the number of predictors is $N + 2$). The

functions must be interpreted together to gain an accurate understanding of group differences. Any particular function may have optimal discriminatory power for any number of the groups. For example, if there are five groups, function one may chiefly discriminate groups two and three from the others, or group one from the others, or groups one and five from the other three, and so on. To see what differences a function is emphasizing, it is helpful to look at the mean scores on that function for the groups (known as group centroids). In some cases, a graph may be used to depict the "space" defined by the first two or three functions.

The standardized weights are interpreted analogously to regression weights. The direction of the relationship is indicated by the sign of the weight, and its relative importance is given by its magnitude. Interpretation of discriminant weights is subject to the same distortions as for regression, but in most cases the magnitude of the weight is a reasonable index of relative importance, provided that small differences are ignored.

There is no direct equivalent to R-squared for discriminant analysis. It is possible, however, to calculate the squared canonical correlation between the function scores and the dependent variable (i.e., group membership). This can be interpreted as an index of explained variance, since it is a marker of the extent to which the functions correctly assign group membership. For multiple discriminant analysis—where there are two or more discriminant functions—this index (commonly referred to as 1 − lambda) corresponds to the explanatory power of all the functions taken together. It is then recalculated as, one by one, the functions are removed. Thus with four functions there will be four canonical correlations, the first of which is for all four functions, the second for the last three functions, the third for the last two functions, and the fourth for the last function alone.

As with OLS regression, the discriminant functions are theoretically significant only if they account for a meaningful amount of variability in the criterion. This is a matter of interpretation. In general, functions that account for more variability are more important. The optimal number of functions for a given set of data depends on the number of functions with reasonable explanatory power—not simply on the number that are statistically significant.

Discriminant analysis makes a couple of assumptions about the characteristics of the data that lead many researchers to use logistic regression, which is similar but does not make these restrictive assumptions. Logistic regression, however, is difficult to interpret, since it involves weights in the form of logged odds ratios. As it turns out, discriminant analysis is robust, and violations of the assumptions are rarely problematic, especially when the groups in the sample are large. If one is cautious in the interpretation of standardized weights (a good practice, in any event), then there is often no good reason to use the more complicated logistic regression even if one suspects that the assumptions of discriminant analysis are incorrect (Klecka, 1980; Pedhazur, 1982). There are occasions, however, when a logistic analysis produces results that are more clear, which is why we have relied on it in chapter eight.

6. Business and media elites, surveyed in 1979, were not asked these questions.

7. The reliability of the *Los Angeles Times* was asked of the television and film-makers, while bureaucrats, congressional aides, judges, labor leaders, corporate layers, military leaders, public interest leaders, and members of the religious elite were asked about the reliability of the *Washington Post*.

8. Since most of the respondents who were asked about this newspaper were television and movie elites, we omitted the dimension of liberalism not available for them (regime threat).

9. While there are significant omissions—such as the *American Spectator, Rolling Stone,* and *Tikkun* (which was not yet in existence)—we believe that all of the journals asked about deserve inclusion.

10. Very few respondents selected the "no opinion" response for mainstream news outlets; these responses could be safely eliminated from the analysis. For *Time,* 2 percent; *Newsweek,* 3 percent; *U.S. News,* 9 percent; *New York Times,* 1 percent; television network news, 6 percent; PBS, 3 percent; *Washington Post,* 3 percent; *Los Angeles Times,* 2 percent.

11. Some of the religious leaders, labor leaders, and federal judges were asked about the 1984 election as well; however, there are too few cases to include here. The results are no different from those reported here.

12. We also constructed two separate indexes summing up the total Democratic and total Republican votes. When looking at both individual elections, and Democratic versus Republican totals, the three ideological dimensions explain about 45 percent of the variance. Collectivist liberalism had the largest standardized coefficient, followed by expressive individualism and system alienation (results not shown here).

Chapter 5: The Components of Collectivist Liberalism

1. Our account relies heavily on several major secondary sources, including Eric Goldman's account of "reform Darwinism" (1952), Morton White's discussion of the attack on formalism (1949), and Sidney Fine's study of the growth of the idea of the welfare state (1956). Each of these works examines, albeit from slightly different angles, "the dissolving [of] the steel chain of ideas" of the earlier conservatism (Goldman, 1952, p. 85) and its replacement by liberal progressive thought as the dominant ethos of American intellectuals. The label "liberal progressivism" seems the most convenient. While other labels such as Goldman's "reform Darwinism" and White's "anti-formalism" capture important aspects of liberal progressive thought, they underplay the importance of the instrumentalist social reform orientation that was part and parcel of the movement and of the work and public activities of such major influential intellectual figures as Charles A. Beard, Thorstein Veblen, and above all, John Dewey.

Although liberal progressivism became the dominant ethos among the intelligentsia, there were always a few dissidents. Not only did Communism enjoy much sympathy during the Depression years (see, e.g., Lyons, 1941; Aaron, 1961; Hook, 1987; Schlesinger, 1988), but conservative critics such as Walter Lippmann, H. L. Mencken, Frank Knight, and Albert J. Nock were eloquent and active. Nonetheless, historian George Nash (1976) is correct in portraying this period as the nadir in the influence of conservative intellectual thought in America.

2. One of the Sumner's essays, as relevant today as when it was written, is entitled "The Absurd Effort to Make the World Over" (Sumner, 1963).

3. Merle Curti, a liberal-progressive historian and author of the leading high school history textbook of the 1940s and 1950s, described Harris's political views rather condescendingly. Curti objected to Harris, claiming that he "ignored the possibility of an increase in the total national income of a socialist state" (Curti, 1959, p. 327).

4. Historian Lawrence Cremin (1988) claims that Harris's philosophy was "obsolete" even before he left the office of education commissioner. Cremin does admit to "a radical nobility about Harris's insistence that men and women of all classes were educable and that properly schooled, they would create a popular culture worthy of the finest aspirations of the founders of the Republic" (p. 164). Compare this with a remark by

Diane Ravitch, former assistant secretary of education: "I strongly believe that all children who are capable of learning should receive a broad liberal education during their years in school. . . . I would like to see all children meet real standards of achievement in history, literature, science, mathematics, and foreign language" (1983, pp. 14, 16).

5. In addition to the critiques offered by Hofstadter and White, Samuel Eliot Morison's presidential address to the American Historical Association (1951) offers a pointed critique of Charles A. Beard (pp. 265–69).

6. The formula remained useful enough for Dr. Martin Luther King, Jr., to invoke successfully in support of black civil rights, "I have a dream that one day my children will be judged according to the content of their character and not the color of their skin" (quoted in Ravitch, 1990, p. 333).

7. Dewey's democratic socialism is rarely stressed in discussions of his philosophy. Analyses usually focus on his more technical epistemological and methodological arguments (e.g., Schlipp and Hahn, 1989). Socialism nonetheless played an important role in Dewey's thought throughout his life. Despite his emphasis on experimentalism, Dewey assumed that a socialist experiment carried no risks of failure (e.g., Geiger, 1989; Damico, 1978; Westbrook, 1991).

8. Additional references to Dewey's socialism in his work include the following: In *Liberalism and Social Action,* a work Sidney Hook once proclaimed to be to the twentieth century what the Communist Manifesto was to the nineteenth century (quoted in Westbrook, 1991, p. 463), Dewey makes the following statements: "[We should] socialize the forces of production" (p. 88); "We should through organized endeavor institute the socialized economy"; the "socialized economy is the means of free individual development as the end" (p. 90). He also claims we should "seek to attain the inclusive end of a socialized economy" (p. 91); and also, "by concentrating upon the task of securing a socialized economy as the ground and medium for release of the impulses and capacities men agree to call ideal, the now scattered and often conflicting activities of liberals can be brought to effective unity" (p. 91). In *Individualism Old and New,* Dewey claims that "'socialization'. . . marks the beginning of a new era of integration" (p. 48), and "a stable recovery of individuality waits upon an elimination of the older economic and political individualism" (p. 72); he further proclaims that "the future historian will combine admiration of those who had the imagination first to see that the resources of technology might be directed by organized planning to serve chosen ends with astonishment at the intellectual and moral hebetude of other peoples who were technically much further advanced" (p. 95). Dewey has an entire chapter entitled "Capitalistic or Public Socialism?" (pp. 101–20), including a startling example of historical absolutism: "We are in for some kind of socialism. . . . Economic determinism is now a fact, not a theory" (p. 119). The same dogmatic point of view is revealed in Dewey's articles in the *Social Frontier,* where for several years he had a regular column. Dewey stated in an unpublished lecture given in China in 1919: "Socialism, no matter what its shade, is centered on the one concept of the welfare of the total society, and this rather than individual profit should be the criterion according to which economic organization and economic enterprise are judged" (quoted in Westbrook, 1991, p. 249). Westbook provides evidence that Dewey's socialism was not merely academic—his actions included voting for the Socialist party numerous times in both presidential and local elections, participating in the founding of the socialist League for Industrial Democracy, and, during the 1930s, organizing the short-lived socialist League for Independent Political Action (see Westbrook, 1991, pp. 277–78, 429–62).

9. Clearly, Dewey, Beard, and others committed the fallacy of foisting moral judgments on supposedly inevitable trends. Philosopher Kenneth Minogue calls this phenomenon "trend persuasion" or "making trends and influencing people" (1963). Isaiah Berlin and Karl Popper have made strong arguments to this effect (see Popper's *Poverty of Historicism*, 1960, and Berlin's memorable essay on historical determinism, 1969). Berlin states that letting "history" make moral judgments is not a viable substitute for individual reflection and determination. Even if some event is the "wave of the future," one still has a choice of whether or not to oppose it. Popper makes the point that talk of "inevitable trends" is a form of social metaphysics or prophesying that is not subject to scientific test. Moreover, strictly speaking, he argues that there are no deterministic laws of history. According to Popper, scientific laws take the form of conditional statements rather than of absolutes. For example, if the price of a commodity rises, then demand for it decreases. Both of these objections are telling against a philosophy like Dewey's, which places great stock in its compatibility with scientific inquiry (e.g., Westbrook, 1991).

10. An excellent example of how this vision is made manifest is given in Mario Cuomo's famous keynote address to the 1984 Democratic National Convention, "A Tale of Two Cities" (Cuomo, 1984).

11. Eighty percent of mainline Protestant religious leaders and 81 percent of Democratic congressional aides identify themselves as liberal.

12. We combined mothers' and fathers' views into two different indexes. The first was the sum of fathers' and mothers' views, the second the product of mothers' and fathers' views. The rationale for the second index is that the impact of parental views should be greater when they are in agreement than otherwise. The results for the additive index were close to those of mothers' views, while the results of using the multiplicative index closely approximated those for fathers' political views.

13. Respondents were asked to characterize the income level of their family at the time they were growing up on a five-point scale, where one is well below average, three is average, and five is well above average. The amount of education respondents received is measured by a seven-point scale where one is some high school and seven is a graduate degree.

Our analysis relies on a stepwise regression, a variation of ordinary regression that emphasizes the relative contribution of a predictor or set of predictors. It is ordinary regression done in two (or more) stages. First an equation is calculated without the variable or variables of interest. Then the equation is recalculated with all the predictors and the change in the explanatory power (as measured by R-squared) recorded. The change in R-squared is used with a comparison of the size of the standardized coefficients to formulate the relative importance of the predictors of interest. The standardized coefficients displayed in the tables of stepwise analyses are for the final equation—that is, the one with all of the variables added. The weights are interpreted in exactly the same way as ordinary regression.

The R-squared value displayed is for the final equation. It, too, is interpreted in the manner of ordinary regression. In addition to the overall R-squared, there is an entry labeled "change in R-squared." This represents the increase in the explanatory power of the equation when the variable of interest is entered. Thus, the amount of change serves an index of the relative importance of the variable of interest, in the context of the other predictors.

Mathematically, stepwise regression is not different from ordinary regression. The only advantage is that it provides a direct assessment of the relative value of the variable of interest. The value of the change in R-squared is a better indicator of relative importance than the magnitude of the standardized weight.

Chapter 6: Expressive Individualism, Religion, and the Family

1. Compare the statement in *Hamlet* spoken by Polonius: "This above all: to thine own self be true. And it must follow, as the night the day, thou canst not then be false to any man." For Shakespeare, Polonius is the fool, not the prophet. The traditional American sentiment is well-expressed in the popular song "America the Beautiful": "Confirm thy soul in self-control, Thy liberty in law!"

2. Benedict's work is famous for its promotion of cultural relativity, but less acknowledged is her proposed practical use for this doctrine: "The recognition of cultural relativity carries with it its own values, which need not be those of the absolutist philosophies." Once this is accepted we will possess "a more realistic social faith accepting . . . the coexisting and equally valid patterns of life" (Benedict, 1934, p. 278). It is of direct relevance here that Benedict explicitly compares the "rigid" treatment of homosexuality in America with a more functional view of it taken by the Zuni and other Native American tribes (pp. 262–65).

3. Sanger herself provided the future platform for promoting emancipationist impulses with her subsequent attacks on criminal sanctions not only on contraception and abortion but also illegitimacy, including "the right to be an unmarried mother" (Chesler, 1992, pp. 98–99).

4. Religious leaders are sharply split. While 95 percent of fundamentalists think homosexual relations are wrong, only 76 percent of Catholic leaders and 58 percent of mainline Protestant leaders feel similarly. Hunter reports similar findings among religious leaders (1991, p. 340).

5. All the results reported here were computed in two distinct ways—first without the occupational dummy variables, and second with them included. Table 6.1 reports the second, more complete equation. This differential procedure allows us to separate out two processes: testing for spuriousness and testing for an intervening occupational effect. Only the inclusion of other background variables is a proper test of the first. The occupational dummy variables are, if statistically significant, intervening variables. While membership in one of these groups cannot be said to cause race, sex, age, ethnicity, fathers' occupational classification, family income of respondents' parents, or respondents' education, differences in these variables among respondents are likely to influence career choice and thus occupational membership.

6. Respondents were asked for their state of origin or, if foreign born, country of origin. We collapsed the results into regional categories: Northeast, South, Midwest, West, and foreign born.

7. The few Unitarians ($N = 11$), Quakers ($N = 8$), Mormons ($N = 8$), Greek Orthodox ($N = 13$), Hindus, Muslims, and Buddhists ($N = 20$) were omitted from the analysis.

8. Religious affiliation is treated as a dummy variable, with Protestant as the reference category. This purely arbitrary selection does not affect either the relatively large proportion of the variance explained by religion or the statistical significance of any of the individual differences.

9. Catholics are statistically significantly more conservative than their Protestant counterparts. This Catholic-Protestant gap is paralleled among differing groups of Chris-

tian religious leaders. Mainline Protestant leaders, who average 95.76, are significantly more liberal than both fundamentalists, who average 85.74, and Catholic religious leaders, who average 88.76. There is no statistically significant difference between fundamentalist and Catholic religious leaders, perhaps because of the small sample size. It is also of interest to compare religious leaders with the laity. Mainline Protestant religious leaders, at 95.76, are more conservative than Protestant elites in other occupations, who have a mean score of 97.54. Catholic elites, at 85.74, are considerably more conservative than their lay elite counterparts, who average 93.37. While the overwhelming majority of the Protestants in our other elite samples appear to be mainline Protestants, the gap between them and fundamentalist religious leaders is an average of 10.02 points. Protestant elite members are a full standard deviation more liberal than are fundamentalist religious leaders.

10. These findings are similar to other analyses on Jewish elites (Lerner, Nagai, and Rothman, 1989), even though the definition of who is Jewish is based on religion in this study but on ethnicity in our earlier one. (The data are not presented here in tabular form.)

11. Of course occupations tend to draw people with different sensibilities to them. Individuals who graduate from West Point or who become motion picture directors are unlikely (modally) to have the same attitudes as each other or to be characterized by the same personality type.

Chapter 7: Components of the Adversary Culture

1. For a detailed discussion of the student movement and its impact see Rothman and Lichter, 1982. The theoretical discussion in this chapter is partly based on the analysis in that book.

2. It is true, however, that while efficacy and legitimacy are distinct, they are not empirically unrelated. If a legitimate government is sufficiently inefficacious, especially in maintaining social order and defending the state from foreign foes, its legitimacy will soon be in serious question. Thus the legitimacy of any government that loses a war is usually challenged, and loss of a war is a common precipitant of regime change. The inability of the American government to win the Vietnam War helped greatly to delegitimize its activities in the eyes of its critics. Similarly, a reasonably efficacious government is bound sooner or later to be granted at least a certain grudging degree of legitimacy, a process lawyers have called "the normative force of the actual."

3. See also Powers, Rothman, and Rothman (1992, 1993). The same authors will be publishing a volume on the motion picture industry entitled *Hollywood's America*.

4. The system support versus system alienation dimension also differs from the regime threat dimension discussed later in this chapter.

5. The following additional social background variables are not significant: town size, mother's view, father's and mother's education, and church attendance.

6. We divided father's class status into upper-white managerial, professional, lower-white collar, and blue collar.

7. Sumner (1906) also invented the terms *ethnocentrism* and *stereotype* and introduced the notions of mores and folkways into the English language in his classic social science text *Folkways*.

8. If Inglehart had submitted his data to factor analysis, we think he would have

found a further split between material and safety needs, as we did. In addition, it is not clear why there is an evolution of needs. Persons have spiritual and religious needs whether or not they are poor (for example, the American Puritans, who were by modern standards both poor and religious). Weber, Durkheim, and Tocqueville, to name only a few, believe that spiritual needs are an intrinsic part of human nature. "Materialism" is an inaccurate description of the work ethic.

9. We struggled over the terminology used to describe this dimension. Two alternative formulations, which we rejected, were "outsider threat" and "use of force."

The second factor analysis of thirty questions with eight groups also yielded an affirmative action dimension, which is, interestingly, independent of responses to other race questions. In fact, there is more consensus on racial issues—for liberals and conservative alike—than on any other set of issues we have studied (see Lerner, Nagai, and Rothman, 1990b, for a brief discussion). However, since this dimension contained only questions dealing with affirmative action and did not differentiate among our groups, we have excluded it from our analysis.

10. The opinions of the judges are surprising, given that half of them had been appointed by Democratic presidents and had voted consistently for Democrats.

11. The following table compares factor loadings as suggested by Marradi (1981) (see appendix for questionnaire codes).

Factor Loadings of Regime Threat on Combined Elite Sample

	With Other Questions	Alone
V166	0.61	0.78
V185	0.60	0.70
V161	0.50	0.64
V188	0.57	0.63
N = 1,055		N = 1,152
Questions = 30		Questions = 4

12. Our results are summarized in the following table (see appendix for questionnaire codes).

Factor Loadings of Regime Threat on Philanthropic Elite Sample

	With Other Questions	Alone
V166	0.63	0.62
V185	0.59	0.64
V161	0.48	0.57
V188	0.60	0.79
V242	0.56	0.67
N = 111		N = 120
Questions = 32		Questions = 5

When we performed the original factor analysis of the philanthropic elite, we found that a question on school prayer also loaded on the regime threat factor. Since we have only the responses to a single question, we decided to eliminate the question from further analysis. While we dropped this question from our analysis, it is possible that the regime threat factor draws on the American "collective conscience" in a way not dissimilar to the role of American civil religion as described by Bellah (1970). Consistent with the line pursued here is that the only religion value that predicts no regime threat is "none" on religious belief. All the other dimensions of liberalism have a distinctive "Jewish" effect, but this dimension does not. Perhaps it is here that American patriotism fits into a more general ideological context.

13. There are only a few data sources that include both types of questions and thus allow us to analyze further the existence of an underlying regime threat dimension.

14. There are exceptions. The factor with the most predictive power in the case of Gloria Steinem is expressive individualism (p. 38).

Chapter 8: Personality, Family, and Ideology

1. Some social scientists drew the opposite conclusions regarding the New Left, including Rothman and Lichter (1982), among others. They note, however, that the critics were a small minority. For a summary of the dissent, see ibid., p. 52.

2. For a more detailed discussion of these issues see ibid., pp. 52–79.

3. In our study, the coders scored the stories blindly, without knowledge of the other aspects of our work or the identities of the respondents.

4. The scoring system was developed by Jennifer Cole as part of her Ph.D. dissertation in psychology at the University of Michigan. Cole scored the protocols without being aware of either the nature of the sample or the purpose of the study. The scoring system has not been empirically tested and must be used with caution.

5. Two methodological notes require mention. Stories with twenty-five or fewer words were determined by professional coders too short to score, and each motive score was corrected for story length. This corrects for the raw finding that the longer respondent stories are, as measured by the number of words, the more highly correlated they are with various motive scores. The correction itself was performed using a simple regression procedure described by psychologist David Winter (Winter and Stewart, 1978). A useful result of this adjustment is that the correlations between different motive scores are reduced somewhat, allowing for more precise estimation of their independent effects.

6. Journalists have had slightly more education than businessmen, however education is positively related to being in business because Hollywood and TV personnel have had considerably less education than have businessmen.

7. In table 8.3 the standardized discriminant weights are interpreted relative to group means. Typically, one group mean is positive and the other is near zero or negative. Larger scores on predictors with positive weights contribute to membership in the group with the larger positive mean, while larger scores on predictors with negative weights tend to be associated with membership in the other group.

Chapter 9: Conclusion

1. Given the pace of change during the 1980s, this statement has become less true than it was when we collected our data. It is our expectation that the new elite study, on which we are now working, will show a substantial growth in the numbers of women and minorities in the ranks of various elites.

2. These academics, such as John Dewey, Sidney Hook, and Charles Beard, wrote

during the 1930s and 1940s for some of the most prominent left-wing intellectual journals of the day, such as the *Nation,* the *Partisan Review,* and the *New Republic.*

3. For a fuller discussion of the historical sources and likely consequences of these developments, see Powers, Rothman, and Rothman (1996) and Rothman and Lichter (forthcoming).

BIBLIOGRAPHY

Aaron, Daniel. 1961. *Men of Good Hope: A Story of American Progressives.* New York: Oxford University Press.

Agresti, Alan. 1984. *Analysis of Ordinal Categorical Data.* New York: John Wiley and Sons.

Agresti, Alan, and Barbara Finlay. 1986. *Statistical Methods for the Social Sciences.* 2d ed. San Francisco: Dellen Publishing.

Aldrich, John H., and Forrest D. Nelson. 1984. *Linear Probability, Logic, and Probit Models.* Beverly Hills, CA: Sage.

Aron, Raymond. 1979. *Main Currents in Sociological Thought.* Vol. 2. Richard Howland and Helen Weaver, trans. Garden City, NY: Anchor Books.

Atkinson, John W., ed. 1958. *Motives in Fantasy, Action and Society.* New York: Van Nostrand.

Baltzell, Digby E. 1966. *The Protestant Establishment: Aristocracy and Caste in America.* New York: Vintage.

————. 1979. *Puritan Boston and Quaker Philadelphia: Two Protestant Ethics and the Spirit of Class Authority and Leadership.* Boston: Beacon Press.

Banfield, Edward C. 1974. *The Unheavenly City Revisited.* Boston: Little, Brown.

Bartlett, John. 1965. *Bartlett's Familiar Quotations.* New York: Pocket Books.

Barton, Allen. 1975. "Consensus and Conflict Among American Leaders." *Public Opinion Quarterly* 38 (winter): 507–30.

Barton, Allen H., and Wayne R. Parsons. 1977. "Measuring Belief System Structures." *Public Opinion Quarterly* 41: 159–80.

Bazelon, David. 1967. *Power in America: The Politics of the New Class.* New York: New American Library.

Bell, Daniel. 1973. *The Coming of Post Industrial Society.* New York: Basic Books.

————. 1976. *The Cultural Contradictions of Capitalism.* New York: Basic Books.

————. 1980. *The Winding Passage: Essays and Sociological Journeys, 1960–1980*. Cambridge, MA: Abt Books.

Bellah, Robert. 1970. "Civil Religion in America." In Robert Bellah, *Beyond Belief: Essays on Religion in a Post Traditional World*. New York: Harper and Row, pp. 168–89.

Bellah, Robert, Richard Madsen, William M. Sullivan, Ann Swidler, and Steven M. Tipton. 1985. *Habits of the Heart: Individualism and Commitment in American Life*. Berkeley: University of California Press.

Benedict, Ruth. 1934. *Patterns of Culture*. Boston: Houghton Mifflin.

Bennett, William J. 1992. *The De-Valuing of America: The Fight for Our Culture and Our Children*. New York: Summit Books.

Berelson, Bernard, Paul F. Lazarsfeld, and William N. McPhee. 1954. *Voting*. Chicago: University of Chicago Press.

Berger, Peter. 1985. *The Capitalist Revolution*. New York: Basic Books.

Berlin, Isaiah. 1969. *Four Essays on Liberty*. New York: Oxford University Press.

Blau, Peter M., and Otis Dudley Duncan. 1967. *The American Occupational Structure*. New York: Wiley.

Bremner, Robert H. 1988. *American Philanthropy*. Chicago: University of Chicago Press.

Brint, Steven. 1984. "'New Class' and Cumulative Trend Explanations of Liberal Political Attitudes of Professionals." *American Journal of Sociology* 90, 1: 31–71.

Bruce-Briggs, B., ed. 1979. *The New Class*. New Brunswick, NJ: Transaction Press.

Burnham, James. 1942. *The Managerial Revolution*. London: Putnam.

Carnegie Foundation for the Advancement of Teaching. 1989. *The Condition of the Professoriate: Attitudes and Trends, 1989: A Technical Report*. Princeton, NJ: Carnegie Foundation for the Advancement of Teaching.

Center for Political Studies. 1989. "American National Election Study, 1988." Ann Arbor, MI: Institute for Social Research, University of Michigan.

Chesler, Ellen. 1992. *Woman of Valor: Margaret Sanger and the Birth Control Movement in America*. New York: Simon and Schuster.

Coben, Stanley. 1976. "The Assault on Victorianism in the Twentieth Century." In Daniel Walker Howe, ed., *Victorian America*. Philadelphia: University of Pennsylvania Press, pp. 160–81.

————. 1991. *Rebellion Against Victorianism*. New York: Oxford University Press.

Cole, Jennifer. 1979. "Narcissistic Character Traits in Left Activists." Dissertation, University of Michigan.

Converse, Philip. 1964. "The Nature of Belief Systems in Mass Publics." In David Apter, ed., *Ideology and Discontent*. New York: Free Press, pp. 206–61.

Coser, Lewis A. 1970. *Men of Ideas: A Sociologist's View*. New York: Free Press.

Cremin, Lawrence A. 1988. *American Education: The Metropolitan Experience, 1876–1980*. New York: Harper and Row.

Croly, Herbert. 1965 [orig. 1909]. *The Promise of American Life*. Cambridge, MA: Harvard University Press.

Cuomo, Mario. 1984. "Mario Cuomo, Keynote Address," *Vital Speeches of the Day*, 50, 21 (August 14): 646–49.

Curti, Merle E. 1959. *The Social Ideas of American Educators, with New Chapters on the Last Twenty-Five Years*. Patterson, NJ: Pageant Books.

Dahl, Robert. 1961. *Who Governs? Democracy and Power in an American City*. New Haven: Yale University Press.

Damico, Alfonso J. 1978. *Individuality and Community: The Social and Political Thought of John Dewey*. Gainesville: University Presses of Florida.

Davis, James. 1980. "Conservative Weather in a Liberalizing Climate: Change in Selected NORC General Social Survey Items, 1972–1978." *Social Forces* 58, 4 (June): 1129–56.

Dewey, John. 1930. *Individualism Old and New*. New York: Minton, Balch and Company.

———. 1935. *Liberalism and Social Action*. New York: G. P. Putnam.

———. 1960. *On Experience, Nature, and Freedom: Representative Selections*. Richard J. Bernstein, ed. Indianapolis: Bobbs-Merrill.

Domhoff, G. William. 1967. *Who Rules America?* Englewood Cliffs, NJ: Prentice-Hall.

———. 1971. *The Higher Circles*. New York: Viking.

———. 1983. *Who Rules America Now? A View for the '80s*. Englewood Cliffs, NJ: Prentice-Hall.

D'Souza, Dinesh. 1990. *Illiberal Education: The Politics of Race and Sex on Campus*. New York: Free Press.

Durkheim, Emile. 1968. *The Elementary Forms of Religious Life*. Joseph Ward Swain, trans. London: G. Allen and Unwin.

Dye, Thomas. 1986. *Who's Running America? Institutional Leadership in the United States*. Englewood Cliffs, NJ: Prentice-Hall.

Ehrenreich, Barbara. 1989. "Mothers Unite." *New Republic,* July 10, pp. 30–33.

Ehrenreich, B., and J. Ehrenreich. 1977. "The Professional/Managerial Class." *Radical America* 11 (March–April): 7–31.

Ekirch, Arthur A., Jr. 1969. *Ideologies and Utopias: The Impact of the New Deal on American Thought*. Chicago: Quadrangle Books.

Fine, Sidney. 1956. *Laissez-Faire and the General Welfare State*. Ann Arbor: University of Michigan Press.

Flanagan, Scott. 1979. "Value Change and Partisan Change in Japan: The Silent Revolution Revisited." *Comparative Politics* 11, 2: 274.

Forcey, Charles. 1961. *The Crossroads of Liberalism: Croly, Weyl, Lippman, and the Progressive Era, 1900–1925*. New York: Oxford University Press.

Geertz, Clifford. 1973. *The Interpretation of Cultures*. New York: Basic Books.

Geiger, George Raymond. 1989. "Dewey's Social and Political Philosophy." In P. A. Schlipp and L. E. Hahn, eds., *The Philosophy of John Dewey*, 3rd ed. La Salle, IL: Open Court Publishing, pp. 335–68.

Goldman, Eric. 1952. *Rendezvous with Destiny.* New York: Alfred A. Knopf.

Gouldner, Alvin W. 1979. *The Future of Intellectuals and the Rise of the New Class.* New York: Continuum Press.

Hanushek, Eric Alan, and John E. Jackson. 1977. *Statistical Methods for Social Scientists.* New York: Academic Press.

Harootunian, H. D. 1970. *Towards Restoration: The Growth of Political Consciousness in Tokugawa Japan.* Berkeley: University of California Press.

Hartz, Louis. 1955. *The Liberal Tradition in America.* New York: Harcourt Brace.

Hayman, Ronald. 1987. *Sartre: A Biography.* New York: Carroll and Graff Publishers.

Hentoff, Nat. 1992. *Free Speech for Me—But Not for Thee.* New York: Harper-Collins.

Higgs, Robert. 1987. *Crisis and Leviathan: Critical Episodes in the Growth of American Government.* New York: Oxford University Press.

Himmelfarb, Gertrude. 1988. "Manners into Morals: What the Victorians Knew." *American Scholar* 57 (winter): 223–32.

Hirsch, E. D. 1987. *Cultural Literacy: What Every American Needs to Know.* Boston: Houghton Mifflin.

Hofstadter, Richard. 1948. *The American Political Tradition.* New York: Vintage Books.

———. 1970. *The Progressive Historians.* Chicago: University of Chicago Press.

Hollander, Paul. 1982. *Political Pilgrims.* New York: HarperCollins.

———. 1992. *Anti-Americanism: Critiques at Home and Abroad, 1965–1990.* New York: Oxford University Press.

Holmes, Stephen, 1993. *The Anatomy of Antiliberalism.* Cambridge, MA: Harvard University Press.

Hook, Sidney. 1987. *Out of Step: An Unquiet Life in the Twentieth Century.* New York: Harper and Row.

Howe, Daniel Walker. 1976. "Victorian Culture in America." In Daniel Walker Howe, ed., *Victorian America.* Philadelphia: University of Pennsylvania Press, pp. 3–28.

Hunter, James Davison. 1991. *Culture Wars: The Struggle to Define America.* New York: Basic Books.

Inglehart, Ronald. 1977. *The Silent Revolution: Changing Values and Political Styles Among Western Publics.* Princeton: Princeton University Press.

James, William. 1971 [orig. 1907]. *The Moral Equivalent of War and Other Essays.* John K. Roth, ed. New York: Harper and Row.

Jennings, M. Kent, and Richard G. Niemi. 1981. *Generations and Politics.* Princeton: Princeton University Press.

Kadushin, Charles. 1974. *The American Intellectual Elite.* Boston: Little, Brown.

Karl, Barry D., and Stanley N. Katz. 1981. "American Private Philanthropic Foundations and the Public Sphere, 1890–1930." *Minerva* 19 (summer): 236–70.

Keller, Suzanne. 1991 [orig. 1963]. *Beyond the Ruling Class: Strategic Elites in Modern Society.* New Brunswick, NJ: Transaction Publishers.

Kelly, Michael. 1993. "Saint Hillary." *New York Times Magazine,* May 23, 1993, pp. 22–25, 63–66.

Keniston, Kenneth. 1971. *Youth and Dissent.* New York: Harcourt Brace and Jovanovitch.

Kimball, Roger. 1990. *Tenured Radicals.* New York: Harper Perennial.

Kinder, D. R., and D. O. Sears. 1981. "Prejudice and Politics: Symbolic Racism Versus Racial Threats to the Good Life." *Journal of Personality and Social Psychology* 40: 414–31.

Klecka, William R. 1980. *Discriminant Analysis.* Newbury Park, CA: Sage.

Koh, Byung Chul. 1989. *Japan's Administrative Elite.* Berkeley, CA: University of California Press.

Kristol, Irving. 1978. *Two Cheers for Capitalism.* New York: Basic Books.

———. 1983. *Reflections of a Neoconservative.* New York: Basic Books.

Ladd, Everett C. 1978. "The New Lines Are Drawn: Class and Ideology in America, Part I." *Public Opinion* 3: 48–53.

———. 1979. "Pursuing the New Class: Social Theory and Survey Data." In B. Bruce-Briggs, ed., *The New Class.* New Brunswick, NJ: Transaction Press, pp. 101–22.

Ladd, Everett C., and Seymour Martin Lipset. 1975. *The Divided Academy: Professors and Politics.* New York: McGraw-Hill.

Laswell, Harold. 1950. *Politics: Who Gets What, When, How.* New York: P. Smith.

———. 1951. *The World Revolution of Our Time: A Framework for Basic Policy Research.* Stanford: Stanford University Press.

Lasswell, Harold, and Daniel Lerner. 1952. *The Comparative Study of Elites.* Stanford: Stanford University Press.

Lasswell, Harold D., Daniel Lerner, and Hans Speier, eds. 1980. *Propaganda and Communication in World History: A Pluralizing World in Formation.* Vol. 3. Honolulu: University of Press of Hawaii.

Lerner, Robert, Althea K. Nagai, and Stanley Rothman. 1989. "Marginality and Liberalism Among Jewish Elites." *Public Opinion Quarterly* 53 (fall): 330–52.

———. 1990a. "Abortion and Social Change in America." *Society* 27: 8–15.

———. 1990b. "Elite Dissensus and Its Origins." *Journal of Political and Military Sociology* 18: 25–39.

———. 1991. "Elite vs. Mass Opinion: Another Look at a Classic Relationship." *International Journal of Public Opinion Research* 3, 1: 1–31.

———. 1995. *Molding the Good Citizen: The Politics of High School History Texts.* Westport, CT: Greenwood/Praeger.

Levine, Donald N. 1965. *Wax and Gold.* Chicago: University of Chicago Press.

Lichter, S. Robert, Stanley Rothman, and Linda S. Lichter. 1986. *The Media Elite.* Bethesda, MD: Adler and Adler.

Lieske, Joel. 1991. "Cultural Issues and Images in the 1988 Presidential Campaign: Why the Democrats Lost—Again!" *PS: Political Science and Politics* 24, 2: 180–87.

Lindbergh, Anne Morrow. 1940. *The Wave of the Future: A Confession of Faith.* New York: Harcourt, Brace.

Lipset, Seymour Martin. 1981 [orig. 1959]. *Political Man*. Expanded edition. Baltimore: Johns Hopkins University Press.

Lowi, Theodore J. 1969. *The End of Liberalism: Ideology, Policy, and the Crisis of Public Authority*. New York: Norton.

Luker, Kristen. 1984. *Abortion and the Politics of Motherhood*. Berkeley: University of California Press.

Lyons, Eugene. 1941. *The Red Brigade*. Indianapolis: Bobbs-Merrill.

Macy, Michael W. 1988. "New Class Dissent Among Social-Cultural Specialists: The Effects of Occupational Self-Direction and Location in the Public Sector." *Sociological Forum* 3, 3: 325–56.

Mannheim, Karl. 1971. *From Karl Mannheim*. Kurt H. Wolff, trans. and ed. New York: Oxford University Press.

Marradi, Alberto. 1981. "Factor Analysis as an Aid in the Formation and Refinement of Empirically Useful Concepts." In David J. Jackson and Edgar F. Borgatta, eds., *Factor Analysis and Measurement in Sociological Research: A Multi-Dimensional Approach*. Beverly Hills, CA: Sage, pp. 11–49.

Maslow, Abraham H. 1970. *Motivation and Personality*. 2d ed. New York: Harper and Row.

McAdams, Dan P. 1980. "A Thematic Coding System for the Intimacy Motive." *Journal of Research in Personality* 14: 413–32.

———. 1982. "Experiences of Intimacy and Power: Relationships Between Social Motives and Autobiographical Memory." *Journal of Personality and Social Psychology* 42: 292–302.

———. 1988. *Intimacy and the Life Story*. New York: Guilford Press.

———. 1989. *The Need to Be Close*. New York: Doubleday.

McAdams, Dan P., Stanley Rothman, and S. Robert Lichter. 1982. "Motivational Profiles: A Study of Former Political Radicals and Politically Moderate Adults." *Personality and Social Psychology Bulletin* 8 (December): 593–603.

McAdams, John. 1987. "Testing the Theory of the New Class." *Sociological Quarterly* 28, 1: 23–48.

McCann, Michael W. 1986. *Taking Reform Seriously*. Ithaca: Cornell University Press.

McClelland, David. 1961. *The Achieving Society*. New York: Van Nostrand.

———. 1975. *Power: The Inner Experience*. New York: Halstead Press.

McClelland, David, and David Winter. 1969. *Motivating Economic Achievement*. New York: Free Press.

McClosky, Herbert, and John Zaller. 1984. *The American Ethos: Public Attitudes Toward Capitalism and Democracy*. Cambridge, MA: Harvard University Press.

McCraw, Thomas K. 1985. "The New Deal and the Mixed Economy." In Harvard Sitkoff, ed., *Fifty Years Later: The New Deal Evaluated*. Philadelphia: Temple University Press, pp. 37–67.

Medved, Michael. 1992. *Hollywood vs. America: Popular Culture and the War on Traditional Values*. New York: HarperCollins.

Meisel, James H. 1962. *The Myth of the Ruling Class*. Ann Arbor: University of Michigan Press.

Michels, Robert. 1958. *Political Parties*. Glencoe, IL: Free Press.

Mill, John Stuart. 1972 [orig. 1861]. *Considerations on Representative Government*. H. B. Acton, ed. London: J. M. Dent.

———. 1947 [orig. 1859]. *On Liberty*. New York: Appleton-Century-Crofts.

Mills, C. Wright. 1956. *The Power Elite*. New York: Oxford University Press.

Minogue, Kenneth R. 1963. *The Liberal Mind*. New York: Vintage.

Morison, Samuel Eliot. 1951. "Faith of a Historian." *American Historical Review* 56 (January): 261–75.

Mosca, Gaetano. 1939. *The Ruling Class*. New York: McGraw-Hill.

Moynihan, Daniel P. 1975. *Coping: On the Practice of Government*. New York: Vintage.

Nagai, Althea, Robert Lerner, and Stanley Rothman. 1991. *The Culture of Philanthropy: Foundations and Public Policy*. Washington, DC: Capital Research Center.

———. 1994. *Giving for Social Change: Foundations, Public Policy and the American Political Agenda*. Westport, CT: Praeger.

Nash, George. 1976. *The Conservative Intellectual Movement in America Since 1945*. New York: Basic Books.

Neter, John, William Wasserman, and G. A. Whitmore. 1973. *Fundamental Statistics for Business and Economics*. Abridged 4th ed. Boston: Allyn and Bacon.

Neuman, W. Russell. 1986. *The Paradox of Mass Politics: Knowledge and Opinion in the American Electorate*. Cambridge, MA: Harvard University Press.

Nie, Norman, Sidney Verba, and John R. Petrocik. 1976. *The Changing American Voter*. Cambridge, MA: Harvard University Press.

Nisbet, Robert. 1972. "Introduction: The Problem of Social Change." In Robert Nisbet, ed., *Social Change*. New York: Harper and Row.

Pareto, Vilfredo. 1966. *Sociological Writings*. New York: Praeger.

Parry, Geraint. 1969. *Political Elites*. London: Allen and Unwin.

Parsons, Talcott. 1968. *Structure of Social Action*. New York: Free Press.

Parsons, Wayne. 1976. "Political Attitudes of American Elites: Cleavages, Consensus, and Conflict." Dissertation, Department of Political Science, Columbia University.

Pedhazur, Elazar J. 1982. *Multiple Regression in Behavioral Research*. New York: Holt Rinehart Winston.

Polenberg, Richard. 1982. "The Second Victory of Anthony Comstock." *Society* 19 (May/June): 32–38.

Political Psychology. 1994. "Special Symposium on Political Psychology or Politicized Psychology" (a series of articles). *Political Psychology* 15, 3: 509–77.

Polsby, Nelson. 1963. *Community Power and Political Theory*. New Haven: Yale University Press.

Popper, Karl Raimund. 1960. *The Poverty of Historicism*. New York: Basic Books.

Powers, Stephen P., David J. Rothman, and Stanley Rothman. 1992. "Hollywood History and the Politics of Motion Pictures." In Stanley Rothman, ed., *The Mass Media in Liberal Democratic Societies*. New York: Paragon House, pp. 267–303.

———. 1993. "Transformation of Gender Roles in Hollywood Movies: 1946–90." *Political Communication* 10, 3: 259–83.

———. 1996. *Hollywood's America: Social and Political Themes in Motion Pictures.* Boulder CO: Westview Press.

Putnam, Robert D. 1976. *The Comparative Study of Political Elites.* Englewood Cliffs, NJ: Prentice Hall.

Ravitch, Diane. 1983. *The Troubled Crusade: American Education, 1945–1980.* New York: Basic Books.

———. 1990. *The American Reader: Words That Moved a Nation.* New York: HarperCollins.

Rhodes, James Ford. 1928. *History of the United States from the Compromise of 1850 to the End of the Roosevelt Administration.* 4 vols. New York: MacMillan.

Rorty, Richard. 1994. "The Unpatriotic Academy." *New York Times,* February 13, p. E15.

Rose, Arnold. 1967. *The Power Structure: Political Process in American Society.* New York: Oxford University Press.

Rothman, Stanley. 1970. *European Society and Politics.* Indianapolis: Bobbs-Merrill.

———. 1979. "The Mass Media in Post-Industrial Society." In S. M. Lipset, ed., *The Third Century: America as a Post-Industrial Society.* Stanford: Hoover Institution Press, Stanford University, pp. 345–88.

———. 1984. "Ideology, Authoritarianism, and Mental Health." *Political Psychology* 5 (fall): 341–63.

———. 1992a. "The Development of the Mass Media." In Stanley Rothman, ed., *The Mass Media in Liberal Democratic Societies.* New York: Paragon House, pp. 37–73.

———. 1992b. "Liberalism and the Decay of the American Political Economy." *Journal of Socio-Economics* 21, 4 (1992): 277–301.

Rothman, Stanley, and S. Robert Lichter. 1980. "Personality Development and Political Dissent: A Reassessment of the New Left." *Journal of Political and Military Sociology* 8 (fall): 191–204.

———. 1982. *Roots of Radicalism: Jews, Christians, and the New Left.* New York: Oxford University Press.

———. 1984. "Personality, Ideology, and World View: A Comparison of Media and Business Elites." *British Journal of Political Science* 15: 5–12.

———. 1987. "Elite Ideology and Risk Perception in Nuclear Energy Policy." *American Political Science Review* 81: 383–404.

Rothman, Stanley, S. Robert Lichter, and Linda S. Lichter. 1992. "Television's America." In Stanley Rothman, ed., *The Mass Media in Liberal Democratic Societies.* New York: Paragon House, pp. 221–66.

———. Forthcoming. *Elites in Conflict.*

Rotunda, Ronald. 1986. *The Politics of Language: Liberalism as Word and Symbol.* Iowa City: University of Iowa Press.

Sabine, George H. 1961. *A History of Political Theory*. New York: Holt, Rinehart and Winston.

Scammon, Richard, and Ben J. Wattenberg. 1970. *The Real Majority*. New York: Donald J. Fine.

Schlesinger, Arthur M., Jr. 1988 [orig. 1949]. *The Vital Center: The Politics of Freedom*. New York: Da Capo Press.

Schlipp, P. A., and L. E. Hahn. 1989. *The Philosophy of John Dewey*. 3d ed. La Salle, IL: Open Court Publishing.

Schumpeter, Joseph A. 1950. *Capitalism, Socialism, and Democracy*. New York: Harper and Row.

Searle, John. 1990. "The Storm Over the University." *New York Review of Books*, December 6, pp. 34–42.

Shils, Edward. 1956. *The Torment of Secrecy: The Background and Consequences of American Security Policies*. New York: Free Press.

———. 1972. *The Intellectuals and the Powers and Other Essays*. Chicago: University of Chicago Press.

———. 1975. *Center and Periphery: Essays in Microsociology*. Chicago: University of Chicago.

———. 1980. *The Calling of Sociology and Other Essays on the Pursuit of Learning*. Chicago: University of Chicago Press.

———. 1988. "Totalitarians and Antinomians." In John H. Bunzel, ed., *Political Passages*. New York: Free Press, pp. 1–31.

Sitkoff, Harvard. 1985. "The New Deal and Race Relations." In Harvard Sitkoff, ed., *Fifty Years Later: The New Deal Evaluated*. Philadelphia: Temple University Press, pp. 93–112.

Sniderman, Paul. 1993. "The New Look in Public Opinion Research." In Ada W. Finifter, ed., *Political Science: The State of the Discipline II*. Washington, DC: American Political Science Association, pp. 219–46.

Sniderman, Paul M., and P. E. Tetlock. 1986. "Symbolic Racism: Problems of Motive Attribution in Political Debate." *Journal of Social Issues* 42: 129–50.

Sniderman, Paul M., and Thomas Piazza. 1993. *The Scar of Race*. Cambridge, MA: Harvard University Press.

Society. 1993. Whole issue. *Society* 30, 5 (July/August).

SPSS. 1993. *SPSS for Windows Advanced Statistics, Release 6.0*. Chicago: SPSS, Inc.

Statistical Abstracts of the United States, 1985. 105th. Edition. 1985. Washington, D.C.: Government Printing Office.

Stewart, Abigail. ed. 1982. *Motivation and Society: A Volume in Honor of David C. McClelland*. San Francisco: Jossey-Bass.

Steinfels, Peter. 1979. *The Neoconservatives*. New York: Simon and Schuster.

Sumner, William G. 1906. *Folkways*. Boston: Ginn.

———. 1963. *Social Darwinism: Selected Essays*. Englewood Cliffs, NJ: Prentice-Hall.

Swafford, Michael. 1980. "Three Parametric Techniques for Contingency Table

Analysis: A Nontechnical Commentary." *American Sociological Review* 45 (August): 664–90.

Swidler, Ann. 1986. "Culture in Action: Symbols and Strategies." *American Sociological Review* 51 (April): 273–86.

Tocqueville, Alexis de. 1969 [orig. 1835]. J. P. Mayer, ed. *Democracy in America.* Trans. George Lawrence. New York: Doubleday.

Transaction/Society. 1993. "Polarizing American Culture" (a series of articles). *Transaction/Society* 30, 5: 11–56.

Trilling, Lionel. 1950. *The Liberal Imagination: Essays on Literature and Society.* New York: Viking.

———. 1965. *Beyond Culture.* New York: Viking.

Verba, Sidney, and Gary R. Orren. 1985. *Equality in America: The View from the Top.* Cambridge, MA: Harvard University Press.

Watkins, Frederick. 1948. *The Political Tradition of the West: A Study in the Development of Modern Liberalism.* Cambridge, MA: Harvard University Press.

Weber, Max. 1930 [orig. 1904–1905]. *The Protestant Ethic and the Spirit of Capitalism.* Translated by Talcott Parsons. London: Allen and Unwin.

———. 1946a. "Class, Status, and Party." In H. H. Gerth and C. Wright Mills, trans. and ed., *From Max Weber: Essays in Sociology.* New York: Oxford University Press, pp. 180–95.

———. 1946b. "Politics as a Vocation." In H. H. Gerth and C. Wright Mills, trans. and ed., *From Max Weber: Essays in Sociology.* New York: Oxford University Press, pp. 77–128.

———. 1946c. "Religious Rejections of the World and Their Directions." In H. H. Gerth and C. Wright Mills, trans. and ed., *From Max Weber: Essays in Sociology.* New York: Oxford University Press, pp. 323–59.

———. 1964 [orig. 1922]. Translated by Ephraim Fischoff. *The Sociology of Religion.* Boston: Beacon Press.

Westbrook, Robert B. 1991. *John Dewey and American Democracy.* Ithaca: Cornell University Press.

White, Morton. 1949. *Social Thought in America.* New York: Viking.

Wildavsky, Aaron. 1982. "The Three Cultures: Explaining Anomalies in the American Welfare State." *Public Interest* 69 (fall): 49–58.

———. 1991. *The Rise of Radical Egalitarianism.* Washington, DC: American University Press.

Winter, David. 1973. *The Power Motive.* New York: Free Press.

Winter, David, and Abigail Stewart. 1978. "The Power of Motive." In Harvey London and John Exner, ed., *Dimensions of Personality.* New York: John Wiley and Sons, pp. 391–447.

Wuthnow, Robert, and Wesley Shrum. 1977. "Knowledge Workers and a 'New Class.'" *Work and Occupations* 10, 4: 471–87.

Zeldow, Peter B., Steven R. Daugherty, and Dan P. McAdams. 1988. "Intimacy, Power, and Psychological Well-being in Medical Students." *Journal of Nervous and Mental Disease* 176, 3: 182–87.

INDEX

Abortion, 88, 89, 90
Academics, 104, 112, 138. *See also* Intellectuals
Activists, 121–22
Adultery: attitudes of elite groups toward, 91
Adversary culture, 38, 91, 119; and elite groups, 31, 54; versus traditional bourgeois culture, 33–34; as status group, 35; components of, 63, 70, 116–17, 137; and anti-Americanism, 100; definitions of, 100–01, 104; during the sixties, 102; factor analysis, 112–19; and perceptions of outside world, 116, 117; in academia, 138, 139. *See also* Adversary culture and regime threat dimension; Adversary culture and system alienation dimension
Adversary culture and regime threat dimension, 100–01, 109, 117, 137; and defense issues, 112–13, 115–16; views on crime, 112–13, 115–16
Adversary culture and system alienation dimension, 100–01, 104, 112, 116, 117; and views of elite groups, 105, 107, 108, 117, 137
Affirmative action, 48, 149n13
Alienation. *See* System alienation dimension
American public: political participation of, 6; educational attainment of, 19; political competence of, 42–43
American Victorian synthesis, 86
Anti-Americanism, 100, 105, 111, 112, 116, 117, 138, 140

Authoritarianism, 131
Authoritarian personalities: conquistador type, 127; imperial type, 127; personal enclave type, 127–28

Baltzell, Digby, 21, 22
Beard, Charles, 76
Bell, Daniel, x, 8, 9, 11, 33, 98, 131
Bellah, Robert, 87
Benedict, Ruth, 87
Bourgeois culture, 3, 33, 34, 37, 101, 102, 111; and the New Left, 103
Bowers versus Harwick, 89
Bureaucrats. *See* Federal civil servants
Burnham, James, 35, 36
Business leaders, 11, 135; and educational attainment, 19, 21; ethnic and religious composition of, 24; conservatism of, 50, 51, 137; and system alienation, 51; on homosexuality, 91; on American foreign policy, 107; on economic structure, 107; on legal system, 107; personality traits, 131, 134–35, 137, 140; sample group described, 141

Capitalist system, 34, 35, 36; critiques of, 73, 74, 75, 76
Capital punishment, 110, 111
Castro, Fidel, 117, 118(table), 137
Catholicism: and expressive individualism dimension, 93, 97, 98, 155–56n9
Charity, 77–78
Civil rights movement, 89
Class boundaries, 15, 16

171